OUR WALK TO ETERNITY

An Instructional Guide from Spirit Answering the How and Why of Life's Everyday Questions

Ken Freschi

BALBOA
PRESS
A DIVISION OF HAY HOUSE

Our Walk to Eternity
An Instructional Guide from Spirit Answering the How and Why of Life's Everyday Questions

Copyright © 2012, 2014 Ken Freschi.

All rights reserved. No part of this book may be used or reproduced by any means, graphic, electronic, or mechanical, including photocopying, recording, taping or by any information storage retrieval system without the written permission of the publisher except in the case of brief quotations embodied in critical articles and reviews.

Balboa Press books may be ordered through booksellers or by contacting:

Balboa Press
A Division of Hay House
1663 Liberty Drive
Bloomington, IN 47403
www.balboapress.com
1 (877) 407-4847

Because of the dynamic nature of the Internet, any web addresses or links contained in this book may have changed since publication and may no longer be valid. The views expressed in this work are solely those of the author and do not necessarily reflect the views of the publisher, and the publisher hereby disclaims any responsibility for them.

The author of this book does not dispense medical advice or prescribe the use of any technique as a form of treatment for physical, emotional, or medical problems without the advice of a physician, either directly or indirectly. The intent of the author is only to offer information of a general nature to help you in your quest for emotional and spiritual well-being. In the event you use any of the information in this book for yourself, which is your constitutional right, the author and the publisher assume no responsibility for your actions.

Any people depicted in stock imagery provided by Thinkstock are models, and such images are being used for illustrative purposes only.
Certain stock imagery © Thinkstock.

Printed in the United States of America.

ISBN: 978-1-4525-9638-9 (sc)
ISBN: 978-1-4525-9640-2 (hc)
ISBN: 978-1-4525-9639-6 (e)

Library of Congress Control Number: 2014907227

Balboa Press rev. date: 04/14/2014

Contents

Preface vii
Acknowledgments ix
Introduction. xi
Chapter 1   Forgiveness Is a Gift You Give to Someone Else . . . 1
Chapter 2   The Light of Heaven Lays Out Our Path 7
Chapter 3   The Light of Heaven Will Show the Way 13
Chapter 4   Through You I Do My Work 19
Chapter 5   By Perfecting Being Human, We Have Perfected an Illusion. 23
Chapter 6   Forget Not From Where You Have Come. 27
Chapter 7   Pray to God for Needs, Not Wants 31
Chapter 8   The Path to Heaven Is Paved with Forgiveness. . . 37
Chapter 9   I Am Always with You, I Am in You, and I Am You 49
Chapter 10 Experience My Strength, Not to Carry You but to Love You 59
Chapter 11 Seek God's Perspective 69
Chapter 12 Through Your Actions, Not Your Words, Others Will Seek Me Out. 89
Chapter 13 Give to Me the Burdens I Seek to Carry for You . . 99
Chapter 14 I Am Spirit; I Am One with God 105
Chapter 15 Reside in the Light That Is God. 119
Index 125

PREFACE

There will come a time in our lives when an event or events occur and forever change us or at least redirect our thinking. This is one of those times for me. By putting into print what I have experienced and heard, I open myself up to a certain amount of criticism. Still I am compelled to go forward with sharing what has been spoken to me. I have been told to do so.

Through these messages, many of the teachings of my chosen faith were confirmed, and the answers to questions that eluded me through organized religion were put to rest. Why does this life occur at all? What is the point of all the trials and tribulations? And most of all, what really happens when we pass?

I have found answers in the messages I have received, and it will take a certain amount of openness on your part to realize the significance of what is written in this book. The narratives between each message are only there to allow you to see what was occurring in my life at the time I received the message; in no way does my narrative add any credence to what I was guided to write. You can read the messages alone and insert your life experiences in place of mine; the meaning will not be lost. These messages were gifted to me, and with the humblest of hearts, I share them with you.

Acknowledgments

First and foremost, I thank God for His light and guidance on this path we call life. On a journey comprised of sorrows and joys, I thank you for the awareness granted to me to hear your messages and to find the answers to the bigger picture of our existence.

To Cathy, thank you for opening up a whole new world for me, a world beyond what I could have imagined, a world we now walk through side by side with the realization that life as we once knew it is not the life we now live. Through this newfound wisdom we now realize our walk together was Divinely orchestrated, and as soul mates, we walk together for a higher purpose.

To my daughters, Lindsay and Elyse, your presence is a gift from God. Through your existence I have been opened up to a whole new world of experiences and knowledge, a world of unlimited possibilities that I failed to see. Thank you.

To Roland Comtois, your abilities to connect to the other side are astounding, and you have validated for me what I have always suspected: our loved ones never leave us, and our true life is eternal. Though I was a doubting Thomas at times, your words have brought me to a place of peace. Thank you.

To Effie Rice and Pat Bolger, your gifts as energy workers have opened me up to the new person I have become. Through your work with me, the day-to-day irritations I encounter no longer dictate my path. I walk through life now with a sense of peace and purpose that eludes so many. Thank you.

To my extended family, who by merely being present may have redirected my path and opened my eyes to another way of thinking, thanks.

To those of you who have chosen to read this book, thank you in advance for not telling me that I may have gone off the deep end.

INTRODUCTION

The writing of this book was not something I eagerly began. How was I going to accomplish this, who was guiding me, and of all people, why me? These were questions I could not answer.

The words in the messages found in this book are not mine; they were only mine to write. I know now that I was and am being used as a messenger of sorts, a channel to receive these messages, to transcribe them, and most of all, to share them.

Those of you who have picked up this book are already pretty open-minded about the Divine. Those of you who have chosen this book as your entry into the study of the Divine, I ask you to have an open mind. The open-mindedness I ask of you I never had in myself, until now. Looking back on the events of the past few years and even over the course my life, I see now that I was being prepared for this task.

In my eyes, I am the most unlikely person to write a book, let alone a book with such Divine messages. I see now that an ordinary person like me is the perfect choice for God to make to get His message out. I do not have a college degree. I am a mechanic by trade. I am a father, a husband, and just an ordinary guy brought up in a Catholic home. Some of the messages I have received do not fall in line with the Catholic faith, and it is not my purpose here to challenge any one religion. I believe people's faith in a particular religion serves them best when used as a moral compass. When religion is used to control, judge, or stifle spiritual beliefs, it becomes a way to force a faith in God upon a congregation. God wants us to seek Him out of love, not guilt. I now do not believe in a God that punishes or condemns or a God that would seek our destruction for not doing this or that. The God I know exists is a loving God, a father who, like me, will always love His children no matter what they do. God lives in each and every one of us, and heaven is a place of unconditional love and forgiveness for all.

The vast majority of these messages were directed specifically at me. They came at a time when I needed them most, and many hold a very personal meaning to me. Sharing these messages, you will see, was something I was told to do. The messages started out pretty simple and built upon each other until the larger message and its meaning became much deeper. Most of the messages arrived early in the morning, much earlier than I would have chosen, and repeated over and over in my head until I got up and wrote them out.

We all question our lives and what this human existence is all about. Why does this happen, why do I have to endure this or that, or more simply, what is the point? I think this book will answer all of these questions and much more. Look at this book as an instruction guide to life, which is mentioned in one of the messages, and just enjoy the Divine as viewed through the eyes of an ordinary guy.

I must start by telling you a little about myself. I do this only to demonstrate that events in our lives, when looked back upon, happen for very specific reasons. I won't bore you with details about my life; after all, I'm just an ordinary guy. Up until this point compared to some people, my life is just a yawn.

I met my wife, Cathy, when I was around twelve or fourteen and my oldest sister was going out with Cathy's oldest brother. My now mother-in-law thought it would be nice for the two families to get together for dinner and invited us over. I was having no part of that. I had two older sisters, Cathy had three sisters and two brothers, and I just didn't see the point in all of this mingling of families. My parents thought otherwise, and there I sat between my two sisters and across from Cathy and her three sisters. Where was the enjoyment?

I was taken aback by one thing though. It was something about my future wife, Cathy. Although she was two years older than I was, I saw her smile and knew someday we would have something. I felt a connection, a draw to her that even now I have difficulty explaining. Unfortunately, at this point I was the only one who felt this draw.

Fast-forward a number of years. My sister married Cathy's brother, and they had two boys. Of course, along with this the two families ended up together on holidays and birthdays. I didn't have a problem with this because, after all, Cathy would be there.

Confusingly enough, we rarely said more than two words to each other. We are both godparents to one of the boys, and my sister, sensing something was up, had me drive Cathy to the christening. Not a word was said between us, but I was thrilled.

A few months later, I wanted to ask Cathy out on a date. I had a couple of hockey tickets and kept avoiding the call. The day before the game, the tickets were right in front of me, calling out to me, and I thought, *What the heck. I'll call her.*

"Hi, Cathy?"

"Yes"

"It's Ken"

"Ken who?"

Well, if that wasn't the needle to burst my ego balloon, what was? Still, we went out the next day, and from that point on I was first and foremost in her mind ... I think.

Three weeks later, Cathy was diagnosed with stage-three borderline noninvasive ovarian cancer. Wow. I was twenty-six, and she was twenty-eight. I had dragged my feet in asking her out for so long, and now this. In hindsight, it was all Divinely planned. She needed someone, and I was going to be that someone. Cathy had one ovary removed and required no chemo. After only three months, we were engaged, and we married the following year. My daughters are never going to pull a stunt like that, I hope. Two days before our first anniversary, our first daughter was born, and two years later, we had our second.

Our daughters were the driving force behind us getting on our spiritual paths. Both girls had a variety of food sensitivities and allergies. Conventional doctors were of little help at the time. They would treat symptoms—ear infections, fatigue, and the like—with antibiotics, not realizing sensitivities to certain foods were at the root of all these problems. After dealing with this for a number of years, my wife had had it. She sought out naturopathic doctors who discovered the root cause of our children's ailments and treated the cause, not just the symptoms.

Of course that opened up a whole new world of health care for us. Naturopathic physicians, acupuncturists, chiropractors, Shiatsu practitioners, and energy workers became our first choice in health care for all of us. Mind, body, and spirit are the concentration of this type of healing. I never in a million years would have considered such alternative health care for myself or anyone else, but my wife, guided by some unseen forces, sought these practitioners out. My daughters were instrumental in the path we now take. Consequently, my wife came home one day and told me she was quitting her well-paying job to concentrate on practicing Reiki. Cathy had received her Reiki master certificate some months earlier, and all the negativity and stress of her current job was counterproductive to her practicing Reiki.

Yes, I was shocked and halfheartedly tried to talk her out of it, but I knew there was no hope. I politely disagreed with her choice but offered my support. Once again, hindsight is twenty-twenty, and it was the best thing she could have done. She is a totally different person. She is more relaxed, meditates as often as she can, and is just easier to be with. I got a new wife without the expense of a divorce. There is a God.

Around this time, I started to become very aware of the abilities I possessed, and it was from there that I was guided to the point I am at now. It was 5:00 a.m. on a Sunday morning, and I was wide awake. What a wonderful way to start a day off. The night before, Cathy and I had been discussing her fears about pursuing a path in Reiki. What would people think, especially my family? After all, to some people, any of the energy work is kind of out there. You gave up a good job with benefits to do what?

Then it happened. In my mind's eye was Cathy's deceased grandmother, and a little farther back stood her aunt, who was also deceased. Her aunt handed Cathy's grandmother a crucifix and said, "Tell Cathy to take this and don't be afraid."

It was so real to me. Everything appeared as if it was happening right before my eyes. The crucifix was quite different from the ones I was accustomed to seeing. Instead of being made of wood or pewter, it looked like chrome. It was as shiny as a chrome bumper on a car.

I woke Cathy and told her what I had seen and that I sensed we would find this crucifix in Mystic, Connecticut, where Cathy's parents had a condo. Off we went, but to no avail. We searched the condo and storefront windows and found nothing. Oh well. I'd been told I had quite the imagination.

A few days later, Cathy was on the phone with her mother and asked her if she had a crucifix that looked like the one I saw. Her mother mentioned that she had a crucifix that had belonged to Cathy's grandmother and was thinking of hanging it in Mystic. Well, that created a little excitement on our end, and we went over to see it. There it was—a chrome-plated crucifix. I was like, "Yes, that's what I saw!" However, my mother-in-law had said it was Grandma's, and I had seen her aunt pass it to Grandma. But Cathy's father validated my story when he walked through the door and said, "Where did you find my aunt's crucifix?"

That crucifix now rests on my wife's dresser as a symbol of faith in God and to have no fear when you follow the path you are brought to by God.

This was the start of visions for me that eventually led to the messages written in this book. I was in my late forties, and my midlife crisis was in full swing—not your typical midlife crisis but a major shift nonetheless. It was an awakening, an awareness, and a new understanding about what is really going on here. I was being brought on a spiritual journey and given the task to write messages and share them. I have no idea from whom some of these messages come, while others it is quite obvious come from God.

The door to this world in which I now live opened rather unexpectedly. I had always, as many of us do, wondered about life, death, God, and our purpose. In the privacy of our minds, we seek clarification that eludes us as we go about our daily schedules.

I had read books by many authors about past lives, communication with loved ones that had passed, and near-death experiences. Wouldn't all that I've read on these subjects be amazing if it were true? Well, I think it is, and I'll go out on a limb and say I know it is, now. At first the reading of such books was entertainment for me, so I thought, but now I see it was more of a preparation for something else. We are guided in this life on certain paths for certain reasons, and when we stop trying to control things, amazing things can happen.

The vision of my wife's grandmother came after the unexpected death of a young person in our community. I will purposely be vague about the circumstances of this incident to be considerate of the family's privacy. The connection my family had to this young person's family was nothing more than that we knew who they were and they knew who we were.

The tragedy that befell this family was unspeakable, and their grief was inconsolable. I somehow felt their pain and in my own way sought an explanation of how and why such a terrible thing could occur.

One night while I was at home, sitting alone in our family room, this young person popped into my head. I thought, *If there was some way you could contact your family, please do so.* I imagined this family sitting at home, trying to navigate through the sea of grief that had enveloped them.

Suddenly my whole left side, top to bottom, felt like it had fallen asleep. The pins and needles I felt weren't too annoying; it was attention getting more than anything. I became a little nervous and wondered whether it was a stroke or a heart attack. *Man, there better be life after death*, I thought. I opened my eyes, and like you see in the movies, this young person materialized before my eyes; it was not like I could touch this person, but this person was there just the same.

I know what some of you are thinking, especially if you have known me for years. At the time this was happening, I thought the same thing: it must be imagination, fantasy, or wishful thinking. I was concerned. Had I gone off the deep end?

After I told Cathy about what had happened, she suggested that I call Effie. Effie was an energy healer we had befriended when our daughters were going through their health issues. She was just as you would expect an energy worker to be: energetic with a ready smile and a great energy. I called her and told her of my experience, and she explained it just as I would have expected her to. That soul was there in front of me, and it probably had a message. Effie then asked me to see what I could get on her own father, who had passed.

"Effie, this isn't what I do."

"It is now," she said. "See what you get."

Whatever, I thought. Off I went into life as I had known it. But my ignoring what had just occurred had no effect on what happened next. Things about Effie's father, things I could not have known, came through. I didn't meditate on it or even think about it, yet the pictures came flooding through. I even came up with the month and year her father had built Effie's childhood home. Also, I was able to describe Effie's young goddaughter and the girl's older brother, both of whom had passed years earlier.

Suffice it to say, more visions popped into my head for others too, and when I described these visions to the people, they confirmed that I was accurate. No enlightening messages, just visions, and at the time, I questioned, *Is this proof that those who have passed are still around us?* Bear in mind, I resisted any notion that I could be a channel for those who had passed, but what was occurring was undeniable. These were my first steps on this wonderful journey of spiritualism, but I was quite apprehensive. It was around this time that the vision of Cathy's grandmother, aunt, and the crucifix appeared.

The vast majority of the messages I have received have come to me in the early morning—the time of day when you're in the realm of sleep and wakefulness. I guess that is the best time for the Divine to knock on the door because the typical distractions of our daily lives won't drown out their attempt to contact us. I have jotted down other messages on my way to work, on vacation, in the middle of the day; verses have even been put in my head while I was sitting at a traffic light. Transcribed in leftover notebooks, on scraps of paper, and even on napkins in an effort to quickly get all that was being said, the messages kept coming. I piled the messages on a desk—a scrap pile of some of the most profound views I could ever imagine—until the completion of this book.

In the three short years since this all started, I have discovered that I don't need to hastily write things out. If I don't, the words follow me through the day and into the next until I put pen to paper.

Over and over I hear the first few sentences, and that is all I need. I start with the first few verses, and off it goes, a torrent of inspiration flowing like a waterfall. I must reread, but I never correct what I write. The significance of the message is not known to me until I read it for myself, and then in some cases, a wave of emotion comes over me.

The messages I have shared with others before writing this book have been met with agreement, gasps, realizations, and bewilderment regarding where I had gotten this information. I give up; I now know from where they come. They come from the Divine, spirit guides, angels, and yes, even God. There I've said it. Now let the dust settle and read further with an open mind and just consider the following: if this is really the way life is and if we just follow the advice in these messages, would our lives be worse? I think not.

CHAPTER 1
FORGIVENESS IS A GIFT YOU GIVE TO SOMEONE ELSE

The first message I wrote seems kind of basic, even elementary to me now, but when I first wrote it, I thought, *Wow, someone is on to something here.* It is not much more enlightening than anything I've read elsewhere, but it is enlightening nonetheless. It started as a dream a few weeks after my vision of Cathy's grandmother.

July 24, 2009—Dream

I was in a class with Cathy. She did her assignment; I forgot. I was mad she didn't remind me. It was almost my turn. I prayed for some kind of help. This is what I got.

Who do you love the most? My answer is myself. If you can't love yourself, you can't love anything or anyone else. The four most important things, in any order, are as follows:
1. Life is our opportunity to evolve, to become better.
2. Problems—there are none; they are opportunities to learn.
3. Souls—as humans, few are capable of such evil, but in all cases eventually humans, guided by their souls, will achieve goodness. Your soul only uses its body on earth. The body itself is only important as a vehicle. We are responsible to care for this vehicle so it can last long enough to learn the lessons we are here to learn. The care of our bodies should never be rooted in vanity. In that sense, our appearance is

not important. It may matter to others, but that's something they're going to have to work on.
4. Earth is our classroom. Even with all its issues, there is a direct connection between heaven and earth. Earth is our training ground. Heaven is part of earth, but earth will never be heaven.

One footnote to the four most important things is forgiveness. You can't evolve until you can truly forgive. Forgiveness is a gift you give to someone else.

I read this message over, and I gained a new outlook on other people in my life. If we are all here to learn and evolve and people are not just here to irritate me, I can look at others through new eyes. Though it is difficult at times, I try to have patience and understanding in dealing with others, but it is most important to make the effort. As written later in this book, God is more concerned about perfection in our efforts as opposed to perfection in our results.

The next day, there was another message. I saw myself in it, and I'm sure you'll see yourself in it as well. This message addresses the way we view others' actions and our responsibility to each other is very important.

July 25, 2009

Judgment of another soul is God's job. Judgment of a person's actions is our job. We have no idea for what lessons or reasons a soul chose to come to earth as a human. As such, we have no idea how to judge that soul's reasons for what it does. We do have a responsibility on earth to punish those actions appropriately. These punishments will aid in this soul's "education." We cannot ignore another soul's actions, good or bad, or we too have lost a learning experience.

The earth is like a pond. Every one of us, no matter what little thing we do, creates ripples in the waters of life. These ripples reach out in all directions, and how they affect others may be unknown to us. We must help others in many ways. It may be financially or through words of support, actions, and even punishment. Only they will know what needed to be learned. Even the one offering the help will be benefiting.

When we leave for earth, we are all given gifts—gifts that are not to be used for our own benefit but for the benefit of others. The gifts may be certain skills, abilities, or insights. These gifts may materialize in the form of money, talent, or work skills. These gifts are to be shared. Know your purpose in life.

In hindsight, after getting more messages, I realized that the word *judgment* should be replaced with *discernment*. I write only what comes to me without giving much thought to the message received in an effort to keep my own mind out of it. As the messages progressed, they became much deeper with a language that was not mine.

I had a short break from receiving anything new, and during that time I took a Qigong class and regularly visited a Shiatsu practitioner—all of this with the intention of opening up whatever needed to be opened so I could become a clearer channel for the messages.

My first Shiatsu experience was totally emasculating, to say the least. I left there after sobbing like a baby. Pat, the practitioner, another angel I've met along the way, said, "That's great. You had an emotional block … You had a release."

I left there planning to never return, but years later I am a regular client, and thankfully nothing like that has happened since. Hopefully she's forgotten about the whole episode.

I tell you about this first Shiatsu experience because I use it as proof that something bigger is going on here, bigger than most of us realize. Energy work, meditation, and the acceptance of the possibilities of past lives are integral in understanding our spiritual connection. Reincarnation is one of the biggest hurdles to overcome, and I believe there is more evidence of reincarnation than evidence in the belief that we spend eighty years or so on earth and end up in heaven for eternity. As the messages progressed, this idea became much more prevalent.

As I said before, I was brought up Catholic; the prospect of reincarnation is not part of the holy belief system. Your religion, in most cases, has been chosen for you by your ancestors, and that's fine for most. If you use your religious convictions as a moral compass, that is great. Unfortunately, religion itself is another form of man trying to control man: believe in this or else, worship this or else, wear this or else, do this on this day or else, etc. If you don't follow the rules, you will suffer the wrath of God for eternity.

This is not the God I ever wanted to believe in or the one I've come to know. Various religions have been practiced for eons, and not one has brought about the peace and harmony our human existence seeks. I still attend church, but I don't feel obligated to attend only a Catholic church. Any place where God is worshipped has an energy that cannot be found elsewhere. All religions have positive aspects, but the one true religion is love. This is an unconditional and all-forgiving love that, unfortunately, I don't see occurring on our planet in the near future. This is our path to enlightenment, the acknowledgment that we are all one and that God is part of each and every person on this planet. Even I have a hard time wrapping my mind around this concept. Future messages would more clearly explain.

So, I've put it out there. Those of you who don't know me are getting a glimpse of who I am, and those of you who did know me are getting a glimpse of who I have become.

Life is constantly changing; we must constantly change. To evolve we must step out of our comfort zones. My life was going along just fine, so I thought, but my reason to be here was not going to be satisfied by staying in my comfort zone. I was being guided down a different path, a very different path than the paths of people to whom I'm related. It is their opinions of this book that are most concerning to me. I don't know what to expect from many people because I have been pretty private about all of these messages until now. Still, I know where the messages come from and who is standing by my side as these events unfold.

In mid-November, another message arrived. It came in the form of a dream, and when I awoke, I just started writing. The words came through from the young person I wrote about earlier who died tragically. The names have been changed to protect the privacy of all involved. The message, though, is not diminished.

November 22, 2009

I was having a conversation with Rob about Sam. Sam is disappointed or concerned that the lessons of his life are not being learned. Sam wasn't aware, but it was the right time for his passing. It was a shock to him, but everything went as it should have.

"Mom has to realize that nothing could have changed the course of events. She has no fault. She has to reclaim the love of her family that she had when I was with her, especially her love for me. Because of this outward expression of love, she raised a beautiful family of souls—that's what we are—and became a ---, a path she must continue. Through her continued giving of love, she will honor my life and cease to mourn my death. I am with her more now than when I was alive (as a human). I'm more alive now than ever. She must welcome my new presence and continue on her life's mission, caring for others as she cared for her children. Through your family you realized your mission was to nurture. Why else would you struggle through --- school? Through me you have experienced love, worry, and immense sorrow. These are all necessary emotions to experience and conquer. You are going through an evolution process; the whole family is. Don't go within; expand outward with these emotions and use them to benefit others in the world. Then I will be released from the bonds of a human experience and fully experience the joy of graduation from earth's classroom. You also will feel a burden lifted and transformed from a weight to God's energy to spread throughout your life."

This message was one of misdirected guilt and of love, purpose, and everlasting life. This message benefits all of us who are going through the pain of losing a loved one, no matter how or when it occurs.

Chapter 2
The Light of Heaven Lays Out Our Path

I spent the following year having monthly meditations with Effie and came up with a few visions for her and others I know. None of them were very profound for the general public, but they hit home for the people involved. Then out of the blue I woke to, "The glory of heaven is purposely blocked from our consciousness." Over and over that sentence played out in my head. Once again I rose early, put pen to paper, and wrote.

October 10, 2010

The glory of heaven is purposely blocked from our consciousness. Its beauty would be a distraction to our human existence. It would interfere with the lessons we must learn in our earthly classroom. Why would we suffer so knowing such glory awaits us?

Only through our spiritual evolvement will the light of heaven be revealed to us. At the hour of our death only a fraction of what is in store is revealed to us, an enticing welcome back to our Source.

As we evolve, veils are lifted. Glimpses of past lives are revealed. Some of those memories are to teach us; others are to motivate us to keep moving forward in our earthly classroom. We gradually understand that there is more going on than the life we are presently living. We've been here before, we're probably coming back, and we know of the Source from which we have come.

Every lifetime can be broken down into years in school: the more years, the more education. We choose how far we want to pursue our evolvement. This decision is made by your Higher Self, your soul, and in our limited intellect as humans, it is difficult to wrap our minds around this. As our lifetimes progress, it becomes very clear to us.

Embrace the level you're at now, don't force others to follow the path you're on, and welcome the ones who stand by your side in this spiritual evolution. We are all progressing at different paces, with different lessons and differing amounts of trips back to the classroom.

There will come a time for all of us when all the glory and light of heaven, indescribable in human terms, will be part of us forever. Whatever form we choose, we will bring forth the light of hope, healing, and love to others still on their journeys to the Source.

Another short message for a relative came through to me immediately afterward, and that one shall remain private. Two weeks later, I received a message of evolvement, what is important in our lives, and God's willingness to wait for us to come around to Him. It highlights the fact that God never turns His back on us even though we may have turned our backs on Him.

October 26, 2010

All souls enter this life at differing levels of evolvement. The youngest souls—the least evolved—enter into a human existence cautiously, with trepidation. On the other side, lessons for them to learn are put in place, but somehow in their human experience they avoid them until the "last dying moment."

These young souls come here with a life of ease, a life of plenty, a life with all the material things human existence can provide. Riches, fame, and physical love surround them. They learn all too soon that this human experience is much more than that.

These young, less evolved souls forget about the reason they came: to become more spiritually evolved. With everything placed before them in life, they have every want and desire filled. Well, they now have no need to pray for anything. Slowly they lose God in their lives. They themselves are the reason for their good fortune, or so they think. They have forgotten about their own souls and why they came.

Luckily, no lifetime is ever wasted or without some sort of lesson or "evolvement" occurring. After a life of plenty, material wealth, and other young souls surrounding them, seeking a superficial existence, they approach the doorstep of death. They look around, and they are alone.

Not being able to provide any material wealth to others now, they have been abandoned. They wait for the "dread" of death to be upon them, but it's kept at bay. They now have time to reflect on their lives, and finally at the "last dying moment," the lessons are painfully clear.

The treasures of this life are nothing, temporary feelings of joy. The true joy in life is finding others who love you not for what you can give. The most beautiful thing in a human's existence is the recognition of a soul mate and the love beyond the physical that it provides.

Now where do these souls turn? They turn to God, the God that was not part of this life. The God that had nothing to give them, or so they thought. Now at the hour of their deaths, God sends His angels to retrieve those souls and lift them back to heaven.

Our bond to God and the Divine can never be broken. We, in our weakened state as humans, may forget our Source, but our Source never forgets us.

Not one life is wasted on unlearned lessons. We are all at differing levels, and our recognition of that is very important to our own evolvement.

The person with the world by the tail is not the blessed one—not yet. Rather, the homeless bum sleeping under a bridge is God's chosen. That soul has been through many lifetimes; lifetimes that started with his or her self-interests, all the way up to a lifetime of misery. These souls have sacrificed all so we can use them as a compass to guide us to compassion for others. The souls with the least are the souls closest to God.

This is one of the first messages to address the material aspect of our world and the misconception that our sole purpose of being here is the acquisition of material things. In our quest for the physical, God cannot be in first place; even so, He stands waiting for whenever we allow Him to enter our lives.

The messages I receive do not come fast and furiously. While this is happening, I'm working six days a week, my two daughters are in college, and Cathy is embarking on her own journey as a Reiki practitioner. I am somewhat amazed that the messages keep coming at all and gradually gain more depth. They all sort of built upon each other and have developed into an instruction book of sorts—instructions on how to view and live this life that has been given to me.

Once again, the messages in this book were directed at me for a specific purpose at a specific time. The messages addressed some aspect of what I was going through at that moment. But after sharing these messages with a few people, I realized the messages can apply to anyone. They are written for everyone. I dated them and presented them in the order I received them to help illustrate the deepening pattern of the messages.

On March 8, 2011, I awakened to, "The energy will pour from the heavens." I dozed, and there it was again.

March 8, 2011

The energy will pour from the heavens. Be open to receive. The wisdom of the ages will pour forth for those who are open. The human experience is just that, an experience, not an end-all. We are like grains of sand with an ocean of knowledge laid before us. A single wave cannot noticeably change a coastline, just as a single lifetime cannot bring about all the change in us.

Over and over we are battered by the waves of our lives until we are gently brought back to where we have come, our Source, our peace. The light of heaven will invisibly raise us from this earth as the sun draws water to the clouds. This action is unseen but no less real. Only those who expose themselves to the light will rise. Like dew in a field, be open to the light and rise to the heavens.

The words in the previous message are words of inspiration, and I guess all the messages contain words of inspiration. I know from the text of the message that this did not come from me but rather through me from a Divine source. It also came at a time when I was utterly disgusted with the stresses of owning a business and the ups and downs it entails. Might I add that this is exactly the same month that I told God, "I surrender it all to you. I give you all my worries. You are in control, and I accept the path you've sent me on. Give me the financial ability to pay my bills at home and in my business."

That was in March 2011, and 2011 was the best year I had in the twenty-three years of owning my business. I paid each and every supplier in full. Ask and you shall receive; put God in control, and everything else will fall into place.

After I told God to place me where he wanted me, the messages came on a more regular basis. I debated whether I should sell my business or persevere. So far I'm staying put, sharing some of my messages with coworkers and customers. It may sound odd, but sometimes they ask if I have anything new to share. I will receive confirmation when the time is right to move on, just as I did in writing this book.

A few days after the previous message, the following message came through, and as with the others, it is about our path, our trials, and God's involvement. This is a short message, but it is to the point.

March 13, 2011

Through the gates of heaven, the eyes of our ancestors look down upon us. The light of heaven lays out our path. Many times we fail to see. We pray for those who have passed, but it is those of us on earth who need the prayers. Our trials and tribulations lie before us like impassable rivers. Once again we may not see a path. God's light leads the way. What seems impossible becomes possible. Our journey is cheered on from heaven above. We reach the foot of the mountain and scale it to the pinnacle of peace—heaven. Our lives have not ended; no, they have just begun. In perfection we look back at those behind us. We see them praying for us, for we have passed, but it is us who pray for them to seek out heaven's light—the light that is God's path to heaven.

This was one of the many messages that imply that the life we are now experiencing is not life at all. True life resides in heaven, and our life here is for our spiritual evolvement. The more we accomplish here in our spiritual evolvement, the better.

Chapter 3
The Light of Heaven Will Show the Way

Two weeks later a new message came through—one of opportunity, new vision, and realization. This was the last message that came solely from who I feel is a Divine being explaining life and how God works.

On April 3rd the first sentence of the following message repeatedly went through my head.

April 3, 2011

When a new day of sunshine lights your path, your viewpoint will change. Each new day brings a new opportunity to see things in a different light. Old hurts, old pains, old views, old mind-sets, and old prejudices pale with each new day. Sorrow over the loss of loved ones diminishes each day with the realization that they have passed into the light of heaven. Things that tormented us as children, with each passing day will be tempered. New experiences, new faces, new opportunities, and even new hurts will obscure the old.

Each new day will bring us a realization that our experiences, good or bad, must be viewed as lessons. They have happened for us, not to us. They are intended to bring us closer to God. In many cases they are intended to change us, change our thought processes, and change our views.

Each new day that God gives us affords us this opportunity to change. We must follow the "path of light" laid out before us. There must be no safe harbor for our negative thoughts, feelings, or experiences. In the light of day, learn the lessons that have been put forth. As night falls, cast the negative into the darkness, and God will bring forth a new day, new light, new wisdom, and a new path that will guide us to the ultimate and never-ending light of heaven.

As the days progress we will see that all our experiences, good and bad, were gifts from our Creator to facilitate our evolvement. To wallow in the past would be futile. We must move forward, leave the experience behind, and take the lesson learned forward into a new day.

This life is an illusion. As children, our whole lives were school, playing, whatever. We never looked beyond our teenage years. As adults we look forward to all our dreams and aspirations. We leave the classroom and see a whole world laid out before us. It's the same with our soul's existence on earth; we're here to learn and evolve. Each day brings us closer to our "graduation." When we pass from this life when we graduate, laid out before us will be the most unimaginable peace, light, beauty, and perfection.

Just a new day of sunshine lighting our path and changing our viewpoint.

This message is telling us to learn from the past. Don't drag events forward into the future and each new day brings with it new opportunity. Always try again—a simple way to move forward.

The next message came from God himself and may be the simplest one yet. On April 26, 2011, I awoke to the words, "Obey Me." I heard it as if it was spoken right into my ear. This time the message didn't have to be drummed into my head as I fought to go back to sleep. I got up and started writing.

April 26, 2011

Obey Me. More pronounced words will never be spoken.

Love your neighbor, for I live inside each and every living being. My breath has brought life to every person. My light inhabits every soul.

Rise higher in this life, not to look down in judgment but to guide others on a path to Me.

I walk beside all. The path you choose, choose wisely. I am the beacon of light for you to follow, not a strong wind to guide you. The path of free will must be walked by you. Present at all times on your walk, I am there to support and at times to carry. I cannot interfere with the choice; the lessons are yours.

I am the light that guides all souls from darkness. Choose to follow the light. Obey My word, and the path is clear.

The right path is through Me. Where there is light, I stand beside you; where there is love, I stand beside you; where there is hope, I stand beside you; where there is revelation, I stand beside you; where there is darkness, I carry you.

I am always present on your path. Seek Me, reach out to Me, obey My word, and salvation will be yours.

I am convinced that this was not the entity that had been guiding my hand in previous messages. The tone, the words—everything flowed differently. I was physically drained after writing this short message. At the same time, I was amazed and excited. Could it really be? No way. Why me? The doubt still remained though. Also, as with many of the messages, the common thread is that we must seek God out. He is there waiting, but it is us who must leave an opening for Him to get in.

Through all of these months of receiving messages, other interesting events took place in my life. One event in particular stands out as a real attention getter. It was a confirmation that I was not losing my mind.

Cathy and I had gone to see Roland Comtois, an amazing medium. His sessions last a couple of hours in a room of about twenty to thirty people. The first time I went to see him, I went thinking it might be quite entertaining.

Well, the first person he picked out of the group was me, and man did he hit the nail on the head! He came up with things about my grandparents that he never could have known. I listened as he spoke to others, and the messages he brought forth were astounding. His ability to capture the personality of the loved ones coming through was right on and in Roland's way, humorous at times. He created a very special night of love, healing, and peace for all those who attended. I've gone to Roland's nights of channeling on more than one occasion, and all were very special. However, one in particular stands out.

He started by giving a little history of himself and then went right into, "There is a young person here who has passed."

I am going to be vague here again for obvious reasons. He went on to describe the circumstances of this person's passing, and Cathy looked at me and said, "It must be Sam!"

"No it can't be. It's too soon after he has died."

"Ask him at the end," she insisted.

Roland allowed one question from each person at the end, and when he came to me, I had a totally different question in mind.

Instead "Who was the person you spoke about in the beginning?" slipped out.

"What was the name?" he asked me, and I told him.

He proceeded to go into detail and describe the exact event and location leading up to this person's death. He then went across the room and started to talk to another person. He typically does that. He'll go back and forth between people. Evidently spirits come through all at once, and he does his best to keep up.

From across the room, he looked my way and said, "Ken, yes, you did see Sam."

Whoa, that was all I needed, not that I was asking for too much, but he validated the vision I had seen of the young person in my family room weeks before.

The messages continued after that. When and what specific days they came through is not important, but I've gone ahead and placed them in the order I received them. The next message is about life, its obstacles, and seeking guidance from God. Although relatively short, it is to the point and written in a language that I don't use.

April 28, 2011

Life's obstacles are not meant to impede; they are meant to redirect. Life's challenges are not meant to defeat; they are there to conquer.

Nothing in this life is insurmountable with the guidance of the Divine. The maze that is life is best viewed from above. From above, the path is clear. Where we stand, we see obstacles, dead ends, and endless choices.

By seeking guidance from above, the direction in which we must go is very clear. So look up, humble yourself, and allow your path to be mapped out from above. The light of heaven will show the way. Your journey will end in your reunion with the Source.

You can then look down at yourself and see how life's obstacles redirected you, and see the benefits of life's challenges that you conquered. From above you now see that the path was an obvious one. Seek out God; He has the best perspective on where you should be, and know that He walks beside you and guides you when you seek Him out.

What a message of hope. Nothing in life is meant to break us, and we have someone, God, who is always there to help us. We must seek Him out of our own free will, and the support and guidance will be there.

Chapter 4
Through You I Do My Work

A couple of weeks later, I received the following message building on the clarification of what life is all about and understanding the trials and fears we must endure. This, once again, makes a distinction between our humanness and our souls.

May 12, 2011

Life's trials, tribulations, and problems are not events in which we exist. They are mere stepping stones on the path of ascension. Like new vistas in an unknown land, events in our human existence should be welcomed with excitement for the newfound knowledge they hold, knowledge that will bring us closer to our Source.

Trepidation and fear are human qualities—qualities that have no place in a spiritual being. Nothing in this lifetime should harbor fear. There is no safe harbor for fear in a being of light. Our human existence is not our goal. It's just our vehicle, the method by which we learn.

As with lifetimes past, this present lifetime shall end, each one hopefully more enlightening for the soul. Do not stand too long in one spot on your journey to the light. Past hurts, past pain, past joys are to be viewed, acknowledged, and allowed to slip away. Carrying past issues is like standing in one spot on a climb to the top of a mountain. It will slow or even prevent your soul's evolvement. Find the lesson in each event, learn from it, and move forward. The path to enlightenment is one that should be taken one step at a time. When you reach the end of the path, take one more step into the light. Pass with excitement for what lies ahead. Welcome this passing for yourself and your loved ones. The journey was successful, lessons have been learned, and more are to follow.

This message affirms that there is light at the end of the tunnel. All we go through has purpose, and life does not end with this life. The journey was successful, lessons have been learned, and more are to follow.

The next message came the day after a quite humbling experience. I was running around the shop, eating my lunch when a piece of food got lodged in my esophagus. Now, anyone who has had this happen will understand what I was going through. You can't get it down or up, and if you try to wash it down, the water hits this cork you've created and flows into your lungs.

I'll say no more, but as I write about this now, I find the event quite humorous. I sat in the ER in differing stages of choking, and a bubbly girl walked in with a rolling computer and said, "How are you? I need to ask you a few questions."

God was testing me all right. I wanted to take her and her computer and roll them both down the hallway. Do you think the friendly little question person could wait until the gagging reflex wore out? Through fits of what I can't even describe, I proceeded to answer her questions. Eventually she went on her way to interview someone who was maybe comatose. I'm sorry, but that was what went through my mind. Just because I get all these messages of love, peace, and understanding doesn't mean I have mastered it yet.

I, at times, get a little full of myself, as I'm sure others do, and think that every good thing that has happened in my life came directly through my own intelligence, skill, or what have you. Why don't we take the same credit when things go wrong? The following message hit me right between the eyes.

June 21, 2011

Pride is a bitter pill to swallow. I am the doer, the provider. Through you I do my work. Through you, not by you, My accomplishments are recognized. Listen to My word, be watchful for My miracles, humble yourself, and allow My light to flow through you. If you must feel pride, feel proud that I love you, that I have chosen you, that I allow you to be a conduit for My works. Through Me, for you, the glory awaits those who acknowledge their place in the dance of life. Be mindful of those in need and ask to be a blessing in someone else's life.

Make yourself available to Me, and I in turn will be available to you. All have been brought here to be servants, not to ourselves but to others. By doing so, it makes you a servant to Me, through which life itself is only possible. Follow My path, for you are but a footstep away from failure. Be mindful that it is I who will catch you when you stumble. It is I who is all.

This message just about sums it up, and it's not a message that we are useless or incompetent. It is just a reminder to all of us that God is involved in all aspects of our lives. Our skills, intelligence, good fortune, and success are not a result of our actions alone. They are blessings from God. We must realize and see God at work in all aspects of our lives. We must also acknowledge God. In the good times and in the bad, God is by our side, guiding us, cheering us on, or at the ready to catch us when we stumble.

We are more than just the accumulation of human experiences. We are souls on a spiritual journey of service to each other, a journey of remembrance, and a journey of acknowledgment that this life is not the true life. The thought that we are born, toil, and in some cases suffer only to die has always been quite disturbing to me. If this is how it really is, then the question of what is this all about would never have an answer, but it does.

Through my life and all the experiences I have been a part of, I have discovered, validated, and in my opinion proven that this life is not life at all. The events that took place to get me to this point of realization were Divinely influenced.

We are all souls in communion with God, but we have lost our way, our wisdom, and our understanding. We all receive messages from God, angels, or guides, and we must be open to them. I started paying attention to the "thoughts" that went through my head and started to write them down.

The language is not mine, and the thoughts are not mine. Clearer and deeper the messages continue, and the vision of how my life, our lives, should be comes in to focus.

Chapter 5
By Perfecting Being Human, We Have Perfected an Illusion

On July 15, 2011, my slumber was once again interrupted. I know that sounds somewhat negative, but I'm one of those early to bed, early to rise people, and was just hoping for a little more time in bed this particular day. This message started with the sentence, "The more arduous the journey, the greater the lesson learned," repeating over and over in my head until I put pen to paper. I am quite sure I've never used the word *arduous* in my everyday life, but there it was.

July 15, 2011

> The more arduous the journey, the greater the lesson learned. Don't live your life going from point A to point B as quickly as possible. It is what is in between that is important.
> Driving a perfectly straight road for too long, you may become drowsy and lose control. The twisting and winding road, although more dangerous, offers so much more of a driving experience and improves your skills. Flying nonstop across the country is convenient, but how much did you miss in between? What is between two slices of bread is what makes the sandwich. A ladder with a top rung and a bottom rung is useless; you need the steps in between.
> Life is the same. There are steps along the way; there are twists and turns, unexpected events, and even undesirable events that take place. It is what the sandwich of life is made up of. It is not birth, exist, and then

death. It is birth and then experience, conquer, enjoy, teach, learn, and evolve that comprise the purpose of life.

We will never reach God and heaven without climbing the ladder one step at a time. If we stumble, we can start over. If you fall from the top, rarely can you start over. Embrace the step you're on now. Gain comfort and confidence, but don't stop there. You must keep climbing, gaining more knowledge and wisdom. By the time you reach the top, you will have the confidence, the wisdom, the fearlessness, and the boldness to open the door of heaven and walk into the light, your home. It was long, it was a challenge, but you persevered. It is always good to come home.

The message seemed to have come through from some entity, guide, or advisor of sorts and not directly from God. All the same, after reading this a number of times, I believe it is sound advice and an obvious way to view life and its events.

The next message speaks of remembering who and what we are, of releasing the attachments to this earthly life, and of the love God possesses for us. Received from spiritual guides, all messages are a little more eloquent than previous ones. The messages continued to get deeper in meaning and clearer each and every time. The following one in particular came when I attempted to meditate using some sort of imagery, and to me, it is quite interesting.

I was walking through a forest on a mountain, spiraling to the top. In a ravine I had to cross, I hesitated. A woman appeared before me. She was ghostlike but real, angelic but human. She wore a white gown that flowed like water. She beckoned me. I followed, and she cleared my path. Round and round I spiraled up this mountain. I reached the top and she led me to my Higher Self. She looked at me and smiled, and then like a kite she was lifted on the wind and rose away.

I then stood there alone with my Higher Self, and he smirked at me. I felt uncomfortable, thinking I didn't know what to say or what I should ask. *Oh, this is embarrassing*, I thought. *I meet my Higher Self, and I can't utter a word.*

My Higher Self looked down at me, almost with admiration, and said, "You don't need to speak. Listen to the silence, the wind, the peace." Smiling, he added, "Listen to the stars."

I stood more at ease now and listened. I heard my name called in the voices of relatives who had passed. I felt chills as I meditated, and I feel chills now as I recall this special event. They were all there; I felt their presence.

This all came to me as I meditated without any idea of what I was going to think about. I just let the pictures develop and went wherever they took me. My Higher Self did leave me with a message at the end.

September 23, 2011

Listen to your mind. Your mind works without voice, without sound. The very thing you need to learn in this life you are prevented from learning. Life itself prevents you from learning only if you let it. The mind must block out everyday distractions. The purpose of this life is not to be human but to remain in spirit while being human. Keep the connection, stay in the light, and evolve. Our bond to the Source—God—should not, must not be weakened by our human experience. More so, it must be strengthened by it. Our spiritual evolvement can only be achieved by putting in the same energy that we put into our human existence. By perfecting being human, we have perfected an illusion; we are spirit.

It is quite evident through all of the messages I have received that God does not condemn us. He is an all-powerful, forgiving, loving, and patient God. That does not mean we go about life with no concern about others and how we treat them or go about our lives with no remorse for our actions. More so, our actions speak more to how far we have evolved and what future experiences we must go through to reach our goal of total spiritual awakening. God will forgive our indiscretions. We must forgive our indiscretions and the indiscretions of others. In future messages you will see that forgiveness is a gift—a gift we give to ourselves. By forgiving others, we not only release them and their souls from a burden, but we also release ourselves from the burden of anger, resentment, and depression that always accompany negative feelings. I am not preaching. I am only expressing the insight I have gained in regard to the messages received.

Chapter 6
Forget Not From Where You Have Come

A month later, I received another message that builds on the fact that we are spirit. This seems to be the most important ideal we must keep in mind. Our human existence is not the end-all that some believe it is. With the realization that we are spiritual beings having a human experience, life and its struggles become more meaningful to us. Also, God does not forsake us; it is we who forsake Him.

October 25, 2011

Remember who you are, what you are; you are spirit. Just as a visitor to another land, you do not become native to that land. You may choose to experience Indian life, immersing yourself in the culture and ways, but that does not make you Indian.

You must immerse yourself in being human, but that does not make you human. While here, you are human in name only to differentiate you from other forms of life.

While living in a foreign land, experience the best that culture has to offer. The same is true for your human experience. Just as you would not wage war on your homeland, do not turn your back on your Source. Your free will is a gift to help you experience the best of this existence.

Without being tempered, free will can lead you down a path of darkness. Forget not from where you have come and forget not what you are, for these memories alone will be your light to find the path home.

Rarely do you not long for your homeland; rarely do you not return; and always you are welcomed back. Travelers on earth, your homeland awaits; spirits living as humans, your Source awaits. Just as the story of the prodigal son, our Father awaits our return to heaven. We will be welcomed, not with a diminished love but with an unending, immeasurable love—a love that will heal wounds from this life, right wrongs that have been done, and bring forth a light that grants us true vision as to what we really are. This awaits each and every one of us, but we will not be brought back; we must choose to go back. Our free will gives us the opportunity to choose the path of light. Choose wisely. Welcome back.

Ah, free will—sometimes I think God looks down and thinks this whole free will thing is not working out as He expected. Then again, it might be working out just as He planned. We are all given choices in life; some are positive, and some are negative, but none of them occur without a message. What should we have done in this or that situation? Could something have been done differently? What has been learned?

We must consciously make a choice when it comes to following God's path. When we choose the path of light, everything else will fall into place. No longer will we view the negative experiences in life without seeing the bigger picture of God working in our lives. All events will be seen as blessings to guide us on our paths of evolvement. I still at times struggle to see the blessings in certain events in our world, and I realize it's very easy to see only the good when your life is going smoothly. It is still my goal to continue to remain spiritually connected, with the hope of fully understanding the workings of our existence on earth. After all, our true life is not here on earth; here we are only playing a role.

The next message clearly brings forth the fact that things of this earth are not things of importance. Once again we are given choices while we are here. We must choose wisely.

October 23, 2011

Break the chains that bind you to your earthly possessions. These serve only as tools to facilitate your spiritual awareness. Controlling desires for material gain will open you up to divine revelations, which we are here to experience.

Realization of what is important comes from releasing what is of this world and embracing what is from the other world—the world from which we have come and to which we will return through our earthly death and spiritual rebirth. Everything of this world is nothing, even our bodies, which are used only to allow us to experience the lessons we are here to learn. Nothing physical passes from this world to the next. Our spirits live on without a physical presence. True life comes from the energy of our spirits and the light of heaven.

This life, one step on your spiritual journey of evolvement, can be made easier by unloading the material cargo we drag around in this life. Bring with you the wisdom you have gained, the vision you now possess, and the love developed in this earthly experience to the other side; for it is only this that will fit through the doors of heaven.

We are all guilty of falling into the trap of seeking new possessions. The new car, house, furniture, etc., seem to be the driving force behind everything we do. Personally, I have noticed this in my own life, and I now live with a little less stress. No longer do I worry that my truck is ten years old, the driveway has a few cracks, or I haven't even bought a flat screen TV yet. Look around at others and you'll see that none of these material things are important. My family and I are healthy, happy, and working. So many others have much less.

We must also be watchful for what we ask for because we may get it. The big yard is now becoming a big pain, and the camper sits idle in the driveway, holding just memories of the fun we had when the girls were younger. Still, I am thankful for all of it, and when I view the big picture, I see everything in my life as blessings from God. No longer will I complain about such things because I made choices; yup, free will.

Chapter 7
Pray to God for Needs, Not Wants

By now we all have heard how the world was going to come to an end in 2012. Doomsday prophecies have been part of our human history since the beginning of time, and we all remember the non-event of the year 2000. Computers would crash, planes would fall from the sky, and the whole human race would come to a grinding halt because computers would not be able to comprehend the year 2000.

Well, obviously we made it, and 2012 was not the apocalypse that had been predicted. As a matter of fact, if you're reading this book, it didn't happen. I'm not putting to question the intelligence of the ancient Mayans from whom this doomsday prophecy originated. Personally, I think the ancient peoples of this world had a greater knowledge than we possess today. Who knows? The Mayan culture may have come to a halt with them laughing about the people of earth freaking out about 2012 being the end of the world. Their calendar could have continued, but they grew tired of carving out rocks.

Seriously though, 2012 is significant, and it has been significant for me. The world as I know it has ended. The views I had have changed, and the person I was, although still around at times, has also changed. The year 2012 was the year of an awakening for me and for others, and this is a good thing. It is a chance to try again, to better ourselves, and to follow the path lit by God. On November 13, 2011, this is exactly what was revealed to me.

November 13, 2011

> The enlightenment of the ages is upon you. Fear and trepidation have no place in this awakening of reality. Your reality is not truth but rather an illusion to keep you from the true reality. You have created this illusion as a form of protection, a needless protection. You harbor an unspoken fear, a fear that you are not who you thought you were.
>
> Listen to the silence of your mind. The souls of your ancestors speak from the light, your guides speak from the light, and I, the light, speak to you. My voice is the loudest but requires the most silence to be heard. Everything you thought you knew will be turned upside down. Through silence you will hear, with eyes shut you will see, and as humans, you don't exist. You are spirit, heaven is real, there is no death, life never ends, and your present life is only a dream that is an illusion created by your humanness. Welcome this realization with joy and excitement. Your realization is coming to you sooner than to others. This is My gift to you; open it and see the light.

Basically this message is telling us to slow down, reevaluate, and that what we think is reality is not reality at all. Those of us stuck in our humanness will come to a realization that life is not exactly what we thought it was. It's so much better.

On holidays especially, we tend to reminisce about the past. Family and friends who are no longer physically with us come to mind. Many times we experience sadness, some of us become depressed, and the joy of the holiday season eludes many. Just the opposite should and will occur if we have the right perspective. The following two messages came on Thanksgiving morning, long before anyone else woke up, and were followed by a Thanksgiving prayer. My guide has made it very clear to me how I should be looking at things. The right perspective is everything.

November 24, 2011—Thanksgiving

> By now you have learned and are accepting of the fact that your human existence is merely a tool used by your Higher Self, your soul, for spiritual evolvement. In our human existence, our separation from God can easily be fueled by wants and desires.
>
> Our egos don't allow us to accept the fact that control of our lives does not come through our own actions. Our sense of control and desire

to control is nothing more than a smoke screen, an attempt of the ego to prevent us from realizing the truth. Why is it that you feel most in control when your "wants" are being fulfilled?

This is where free will, a gift from God, can be a double-edged sword. Like any father, God wants His children to make their own choices. Through the process of making good and bad choices, a lesson can be learned.

For your soul, just as in your human existence, the greatest gains are those you have earned yourself. God could hand us the heavens, but what purpose would that serve?

To further help our souls on this journey of evolvement, God has limited our choices to two things: wants and needs. Life is not that complicated when you only have two choices. Here again, free will could mess this up. Free will, guided by your soul, sends you on the right path. It's not a path of least resistance or a path of wants and desires but a path of need. Pray to God for needs, not wants. Pray to God for the vision to take the right path, for the strength to proceed, and for the support to get you through.

The path of want is a lonely walk. It's a walk chosen just by you, created by you, and it can be fulfilled by you alone. We know now that it is an impossible feat. It would require that you alone are in control of your destiny, and in a sense, through free will you are, but the end result would not be your true destiny. It would be a lonely existence of possessions, none of which can fit through the gates of heaven.

The path of need is your only choice, a path created by God himself. Although a path of trial and tribulation, it is a path to evolvement—a path specifically designed for you and what you need in this life to evolve. It is a path of spiritual awareness, a path of divinity, a path of awakening of who and what you really are. This is not a path of self-accomplishment, although it was designed especially for you. It is a path to guide you to the recognition of your Higher Self and the power of God in your existence.

The path of need, unlike want, cannot be walked alone. Being your path, there is only one presence to accompany you, to guide you, to carry you forward. It is God.

You will discover that it is He who controls all in your life, the good and the bad. His control is not that of an evil emperor but that of a loving father. His control over us is for our betterment. His control is to gently guide us back home. The path of want ends in darkness. The path of need ends in light, an all-enveloping light of true love. The choice is easy. Pray for needs.

November 24, 2011

"God works in mysterious ways" is further from reality than most realize. His ways are obvious—if you are in the right frame of mind. Being spiritual is an awakening to who and what we really are. Human beings are the part we play in this life, not what we are. We are spiritual beings led here to learn and become more spiritually evolved. There are lessons in humility, greed, control, desire, want, need, empathy, happiness; the list is endless. All are governed by God, designed specifically for us and our evolvement. Pain and suffering conceal lessons also; they are not intended to break us but merely intended to bend us toward God. His ways are the ways of the Divine and not of this world. Pray for the awareness to recognize God's messages and for the understanding of His ways.

One of the most fearful events in our lives—death—is not really what it seems. On our side, it is tragic, a loss, a perplexing and scary event. On God's side it is a loving welcome home for a soul whose separation from God and heaven is over—a celebration on one side, sorrow on the other. What perspective would you choose?

November 24, 2011—Thanksgiving Prayer

Dear God,

On this day, as with all days, we thank You for what You have bestowed upon us—our families, friends, and even our trials and tribulations through which our greatest lessons are learned.

We pray for awareness—the awareness that we are souls here to learn. We pray for patience. May we have the same patience you afforded us for others. We pray for vision—the vision to see the path that is right for us. We pray also for recognition—the recognition that the prayers answered are the prayers for need as opposed to want.

We thank You for the joyous welcome You granted our loved ones as they passed through the gates of heaven. As they look down upon us today, may we be enveloped in the light of heaven and feel their presence.

Thank you today and always for Your never-ending presence in our lives and for being an everlasting light to guide us each and every day.

Amen.

That was an enlightening way to start the holiday. Unfortunately, I didn't have the nerve to read that prayer at the Thanksgiving table. The relatives surrounding me that day do not know me this way, or maybe that's my perception. Nonetheless, the first time anyone in my immediate family will see that prayer will most likely be in this book.

Now that is not to put down anyone in my family; it's just that my way of thinking in the last few years has gone from one extreme to the next, and I still sometimes find myself struggling with all of this. To suddenly stand before people who have known me for fifty years and start reciting all of these messages, it would be like, *what the ...?*

Gradually I slip in a few new viewpoints now and then, and I can sense some of them are wondering, *what the ...?* For now I'll have a little fun with it.

Another message came through on November 27, building on the idea that the world as we know it was definitely in for a change in 2012. This was the year for awareness, realization, and life-changing attitude adjustments for a lot of people, especially for me.

November 27, 2011

The dam that holds back the waters of awareness is failing. Some have recognized this event as a positive thing. All will come to the realization that this is an event that will forever change the human experience.

These waters will burst forth, not with the power of destruction for the physical but with a cleansing of the mind. The waters will flow as a torrent though. A change of mind-set and an awakening of spirit will be the aftermath. The thoughts of our ancestors will vanish. Our thoughts will vanish. The veil between heaven and earth will thin. A newfound awareness of who and what we are will be nourished by these waters.

Our journey, blown by the winds of free will and fearful thinking, will find itself on an island in the sea of awareness. Blessed are the ones who dive back in to permanently wash away the old and drink in the new.

Our separation from God is comparable to children moving away from home. They find that they can't make it on their own. Many, determined to make a point and succumbing to the power of their egos, continue on a negative path. The human path has been this way too long. The material world has never, and will ever be, the answer.

The waters of awareness have been held back for generations, and the time has come for this river of knowledge to flow freely again. Although these waters, a gift from God, may be viewed as destructive, they are a necessary cleansing for a thought process developed by our humanness. Do not resist the flow, and follow its gentle push to the sea of enlightenment.

Awareness seems to be the main ingredient for a successful life here on earth. Awareness of who and what we really are brings us to the point of being able to forgive, and through forgiveness we can love one another unconditionally.

Chapter 8
The Path to Heaven Is Paved with Forgiveness

Once again a few days elapsed before I received my next message. It started with the first sentence coming to me out of the blue first thing in the morning. This message was different though. It seemed more as if it was from someone who had been here, experienced life, and was coming through to tell me what life is all about. The words *we*, *our*, and *us* are used again. This made it seem as if I was being spoken to by someone who was more my equal—someone who had passed from this human existence and had come back to clue me in on what was going on. It definitely was a message from the other side, but it lacked the authoritative tone of some of the other messages. Nevertheless, it speaks of our purpose here on earth. It is very clear that we come here for a specific purpose. Knowing our purpose is quite a different thing, but we are constantly being exposed to that which can give us the hints we need ... if we listen.

December 11, 2011

    The secret to this life is to determine your lesson to be mastered. Each life we experience, we come as a teacher and a student. It is said that the best way to learn is to teach. Unlike the classrooms of our formative years on earth, the Divine classroom for our Higher Selves requires complete mastery.

Our Higher Selves, our souls, come here with a purpose. Each purpose contains a lesson, and through our learning, we help others. As teachers, we help others learn, and as students, we give opportunity for others to teach. We help fulfill each other's goals for the Higher Self. Our lessons are mastered when we accept, learn, and teach what has been put forth.

We come to earth's classroom knowing what our lessons are. We've chosen them for our souls' evolvement. We have even chosen how we will learn our lessons, but we forgot one thing: free will. Free will, when mastered, is designed to magnify the positive experiences for our souls, but many times it trips us up. Failure is part of learning; mastery is part of teaching.

Your morning shower washes away yesterday's dust—the past—and awakens you to a new day. The warmth and the light reinvigorate you to tackle the now—the future.

Your past hurts, suffering, and failures are just as easy to remove by seeking the guidance found in the light of heaven. The pain, though not forgotten, has been put away in the textbook of life, to be referred to but not to be experienced again.

This is all done by choice. A gift given by our Creator—free will—when used incorrectly sends us on a path of stagnation. At this point, you don't accept, you don't acknowledge, you don't recognize the very lesson you chose to learn here. Your humanness has taken control of your soul. You've forgotten that you are a soul experiencing things that cannot destroy your spiritual being. You begin to suffer on a human level, experiencing pain, depression, addictions, and disease and find yourself wandering a dark path. Thinking you are alone in this, you try to control, further spiraling down, for you are not in control; God is. Accept that, seek His guidance, and seek His forgiveness, which is always granted, and as God forgives and forgets, you must also.

Why is my life this way? Why am I going through this or that? Your Higher Self knows the answer. Every person you've met or will meet is part of the answer. They have accepted to play their part for your benefit and for their own benefit—teacher and student at the same time. Sacrifices are made by all souls to benefit the evolvement of all souls.

Take time alone to reconnect with your Higher Self. Be wary of the false security isolation offers. The aloneness you seek comes through your Higher Self trying to reconnect with our Source, God. Do not mistake this isolation as an answer or a solution to your pain. A temporary reprieve from life lessons, this time is for reconnecting—reconnecting to God. Everyone at some time during the lowest points in their lives will find themselves with a sense of total isolation, alone to suffer through this terrible experience called life. Seek out God; seek out the light that will guide you on your path. When you do, you will realize one lesson has been learned: a universal lesson for all souls, a realization that God, not you, is in control.

Like a parent on earth painfully watching your child learn his or her own lessons, God has to sit back and wait for you to realize this on your own. He wants to be sought after through love, not guilt or fear. So He waits (His patience is one of His greatest gifts) for us to "see the light."

Finally, our paths are illuminated with the best and the brightest of God's white light, protecting us and removing all anxiety for the future. The realization that we never walked alone, were never abandoned, were never worthless is washed away in the light of heaven.

Now we must carry forward with renewed faith—with fearlessness—as to what's in store, acknowledge our imperfections, and master what has to be learned. We all walk in God's protective light. Our worries are now released to God; He is in control. Our burdens are lifted. Without fear and trepidation, we now must seek out new people, new experiences, new lives; the answer to why, what, and how can be explored. Lessons must be mastered. Mastery is part of evolvement, and evolvement brings us closer to God.

The following messages speak of free will, choices we make, and our purpose with regard to this human existence. Not much is left up to interpretation. The messages are clear and to the point. I've started going about my day trying to look at people as souls. We are all here struggling with the same issues and the same lack of awareness. We all need clarification as to what the heck this is all about. When viewing ourselves and others in this light, we realize that all the things that bother us about ourselves and others don't seem as important anymore. Still, at times I slip back into ego mode, and I must read the words written here again. We have been given a Divine guide on how this earthly experience is to be lived.

Ken Freschi

December 16, 2011

Free will is the tool given to you by your Creator to aid you in reaching your true destiny. To understand and properly use free will, there are a number of things you must wrap your mind around first.

Your human existence is nothing more than a means for your soul's evolvement. You are only a soul; this is not to minimize but to elevate. You only experience being human. Everything on earth is only an experience, not an existence. Death, of which there is no such thing, only occurs on earth. In acting as a human, you have created "death" as an explanation as to why the human body, merely a tool, has ceased to function. The human body is merely a tool serving a function for your soul, what you really are. It's your vehicle in this life, nothing more, nothing less. Nothing on earth is truly alive. A tree standing in a field full of leaves is an object performing a function. Its purpose, on the simplest level, is to clean the air. When it ceases to function, it decays, adding another beneficial function to the earth: soil nutrients.

True life, the only life, is you as a soul—an energy force blessed by the Creator, God. Energy in any form cannot be destroyed, only changed. Energy is ever present on earth. Every object possesses energy, from rocks to trees to water—everything. Your soul is energy, a blessed energy. That is what "life" truly is. It will change states but never cease to exist.

Now a gift from God, free will becomes a tool to aid you on your path of ascension. Choices are many, and when viewed through the eyes of a human, viewed through ego, the choices are beyond comprehension. As humans, we seek to satisfy wants and desires—needs that satisfy the human experience. Many surround themselves with what will serve them in this momentary existence.

When exercising free will, choose from the true position of what you are: a soul. Wants and desires turn to needs. A much simpler choice, needs never to turn into disappointment, what-ifs, or could-haves. Seek what your soul needs for its evolvement. Your many questions can only be answered through the light of heaven. Choices presented to you come through God, and the correct choices are meant to bring you closer to God. Think as a being of light whose permanent existence resides in the light of heaven and the choices you make will be easier. Do they bring you on a path of spiritual enlightenment closer to God? Or do they bring momentary pleasure to your human existence?

Many choices are obvious and very easy to make, such as helping the poor, volunteering, taking a walk in the woods, and experiencing the energy around you. Others are more difficult and on the surface seem to be poor choices. Examining our past actions in this life, or maybe even other lives, can be a painful ordeal. These events can bring forth stress or even illness in our human forms, but they must be dealt with and overcome. Examine the past—without judgment—to learn. Do not relive it. The pain you feel will only add to your soul's evolvement. God could make it all go away, but the lesson would be lost. Instead He suffers through it with you, standing by your side to support you. Humble yourself and allow Him to carry you. Relinquish control to God. Our trials and tribulations are not meant to break us; they are meant to bend us closer to God.

The only difference between a lump of coal and a diamond is the pressure that was put upon it. Accept the pressures in this human experience as gifts from God—gifts that are intended to form you into the being of light that you truly are.

Free will is one of the recurring ideals found in the messages I received. It is a gift given to us by God and one aspect of our lives that God cannot and will not interfere with. It's almost like a test of sorts. We are given opportunities to make choices, and the choices we make will assess the point to which we have evolved spiritually. Guided by our relationship with God, our choice through the exercise of free will, will be the best choice.

The next message speaks to our perspective. Our perspective is everything on this walk through life. How we look at someone or some event will never change that circumstance. What we must change is our perspective in that situation. In a situation in which someone annoys or irritates us, our words will never change his or her actions. What must change is how we see that person.

December 18, 2011

Life's lessons can only be evident when viewed from a Divine perspective. Every event—failure, accomplishment, health, sickness, despair—is a lesson in the making. Seek out the message each experience contains from a Divine viewpoint.

The homeless person, suffering greatly, may need this challenging human experience to realize past mistakes and wrong decisions, or even to develop a faith in God that this situation will soon end and that everything happens for the best. A loved one who is sick or dying or a child born into this world in poverty or illness or a child not allowed to be born at all has a lesson in the making. Do not assume the lessons are for the victim. Do not try to rationalize the experiences others are going through. When your human experience is going well or even perfectly as viewed from a human's perspective, prayerful thought should be ever present.

Remember and be aware of the fact that we are souls experiencing a human existence to evolve and elevate our spiritual being. The lesson, not the event, is important. The lesson can be carried away, forever part of your being. The event is one frame in the film of life, experienced and then gone. This life is just a mere snapshot in your spiritual existence.

Remember too that we come as teachers and students, which occurs simultaneously. You will never learn without teaching and never teach without learning. The victims, as we see them in this life, are never just students. They may be going through a negative experience to aid in the spiritual education of another.

When your life is going in a positive direction and you run into another who is suffering, be cautious as to how you approach your "Divine viewpoint." Even though you have been blessed, the lesson before you may be yours. What is it that you should realize? It may be compassion, empathy, thankfulness, or even a renewed faith in God as you pray for another's well-being. Pray for the awareness to see God's messages in the most unusual places. Pray for the awareness that everything has a Divine perspective and that when viewed from above, life's lessons are easily recognized.

How we view others or judge a particular situation someone is in may really be an opportunity to look in the mirror at ourselves. We must be mindful of our opinions because a particular person or event may have been placed before us as an assessment of our own evolvement. Many times the thing that irritates us the most about a particular person is something we ourselves are guilty of doing. Realize that all of us are souls on the same journey to enlightenment, but we are all on different paths.

The next message speaks of the fact that we have created the life we are living. In the physical sense we are the product of earthly influences. In reality, we have come to earth with specific lessons to learn, experiences to have, and the ultimate choice to include God in all of this once we are here. Of course, our ever-present free will may, and many times does, trip us up. Through perspective we must realize the lesson to be mastered as opposed to falling victim to the experience.

December 18, 2011

Events can only be experienced by spirit. Lessons become part of spirit. Your realization that life, your soul, is never ending brings a newfound realization. Your soul, upon your choosing, will and has experienced many human existences, with each existence, many experiences, and with each experience, many lessons.

You must now realize you have control—with God's guidance—over a portion of these lives. You chose what you came here to learn, you chose the experiences that will teach you, and you chose whether or not you will accept God in these events. God is ever present, but your acknowledgment of His presence is crucial.

As humans, we put more emphasis on our experiences than our lessons in life. Understand the purpose of this human existence. You are a soul experiencing life as a human. The events in this life should only follow you through future lives as lessons. Just as in this life, you shouldn't carry forward past hurts inflicted by others; most importantly, do not carry them from lifetime to lifetime.

You have control over the emotional baggage brought forth from past lives. The easiest method of going forward is to acknowledge the event, take the lesson from it, and go forward. Consciously choose the lesson as opposed to the experience to carry forward in your soul's journey.

As for past life experiences affecting you in this life, a solution can be found in you—in your Higher Self. These negative attachments occur when you experience something and mistakenly forget that you are a spiritual being. Human events cannot become part of a spiritual being. Heaven is your home, and earth is no part of heaven. Your Higher Self momentarily forgot its Source. Your Higher Self lost touch with its Divine perspective. Your Higher Self may have forgotten to keep God in the picture. This is free will out of control.

A reversal of this attachment to an experience is crucial. The negative effects may have been present in many lifetimes, and only your Higher Self has the answer. It is not important that you know now what the event was. It may cause a renewed bond of pain for your soul. Seek in meditation your Higher Self. Imagine a meeting with your Higher Self and introduce yourself to it. Acknowledge the things you are feeling that hold you back in this life. Reaffirm to your Higher Self your belief in God and all that is good. Your Higher Self already knows all this and realizes the connection to God, the separation of heaven and earth, and the definition of true life.

Upon passing from the life in question and re-entering heaven, your soul was given the opportunity to evaluate the overlooked lesson. The answer was presented, and you returned seeking to overcome the event again. The answer eludes you once you return. Over and over this happens until the realization that the answer you seek resides with God. Did you forget Him, give up on Him, or fail to seek Him out in one or more of the lifetimes? God must be first and foremost in your thoughts and actions. Will we stray? Will God forgive? Yes on both counts.

The lessons you seek are gifts from God, not to be forgotten among the distractions of humanity. Success can only be found through God. The direct connection of your Higher Self and God can become the path to enlightenment, and the reversal of darkness in your life will occur through the light of heaven.

The suffering we endure is created by us for us—for our spiritual evolvement. Nothing in our human existence will destroy us. God stands by our side as any good parent would do, suffering with us, holding us up, and carrying us when needed, until the awakening occurs as to who and what we truly are.

Holidays always have a special feel to them. Be it a national holiday or a religious holiday, the time off from the daily grind is a welcome respite. Unfortunately, holidays for many of us have become just that—a day off. Lost in our material world of work and the acquiring of stuff, the point of the holiday is lost. I too have fallen victim to the same numbness that drives us to stores around holidays and anniversaries just to get a card, gift, or what have you. For me, the message of the holiday was lost in a sea of wrapping paper, especially at Christmas, until Christmas 2011. The day before and Christmas day itself provided me with two messages, bright and early in the morning, that sum up life's process, the true meaning of Christmas, and the special gift we all have received.

December 24, 2011

There are three very important and necessary mile markers on your spiritual journey of ascension. You may refer to them as the holy trinity of awareness. They will be reached in a specific order but at varying times for each and every soul. As you progress through lifetimes, these mile markers become more apparent, are reached sooner, and blend together.

The first—realization—is the point at which you realize and acknowledge that something bigger is going on. You begin to realize that this existence, this lifetime, has a purpose. Now more questions arise than are answered. The simplicity that you thought was life—birth, life, death—cannot be explained so simply. You have started to realize that your human existence is actually a spiritual journey. You realize there is more to you than just a body. Something is using your body merely as a tool to attain a higher level of consciousness. You have and are a soul, a spiritual being of everlasting light. Now the questions of how, what, why, when, etc., flood your mind, and your quest for answers begins. Have you now found a purpose?

The next step is recognition. Now recognizing yourself as a soul, you realize others are souls also. The holy trinity of awareness occurs separately and together at the same time.

You recognize people in your life who are put there for a specific purpose. Despite the outward appearance of a positive or negative experience, all experiences are necessary for your soul's evolvement. You start to recognize the people most important to your successful journey. You look beyond the physical; you recognize them as souls—what we truly are. You now recognize a soul mate—someone that, in unison with your soul, has agreed to come into this life to play a very important and specific role to aid in your evolvement.

Soul mates are not necessarily romantic partners in this life. That is merely a human misconception. A soul mate is someone you recognize from the other side as a member of your soul group or as that special soul that has agreed to play an integral part in this human existence. The comfort you find in meeting a soul mate comes from the connection of Source you both possess. You both recognize this spiritual connection and the true love that it manifests. The interaction between soul mates may last a lifetime or merely a short period in this existence, but the effects and benefits of that recognition will last for eternity.

You realize, you recognize, you combine the two, and now you reach revelation. At this stage, answers to questions will be revealed. The "what is my purpose, how will it happen, who is with me, when will it end, and why must I endure?" will be answered. The bigger picture will be revealed. Some beliefs will be dispelled, and others will turn into knowledge. True revelation occurs when your beliefs turn to knowledge.

I don't believe; I *know* I'm a soul, I know there is an everlasting life, I know there is heaven, and I know there is a God. I have met other spiritual beings. I feel and hear my departed loved ones. I have felt the light of heaven shield me and protect me, and I have seen God work in my life and in others' lives. I have experienced a revelation.

I realize life is not what it has seemed. I recognize others on this spiritual journey, and I know God is in control and all that happens, happens through Him for the Higher Good. That's a revelation.

That is quite a clarification, and I view this as my Christmas gift. It is a gift of awareness of who and what I really am, who and what we really are. Now look at someone in your life who has a tendency to, shall I say, push your buttons. For the sake of time, choose one because if you are like me, you can probably come up with quite a list. Now look at this person through the newfound perspective stated in the last message. Does it not change your view of him or her?

By being open and honest with ourselves, we can see people much differently when we keep in mind what has been received in the last message. No longer are people and events put into our lives by happenstance, purely for our misery. Instead, people and events appear at specific times to assess, guide, and elevate us on our journey of spiritual evolvement.

The next message clears up, for me at least, the true message of Christmas. Beyond the religious aspect of it being the birth of Jesus, which I wholeheartedly believe, one very special gift was bestowed upon us. It is a gift we had to receive and put into use for all of us to carry on in our journey of evolvement. It is one word, one action, that is required of all of us, and Jesus lived it every day.

December 25, 2011

What is the true meaning of Christmas? Ask any Christian, and he or she will say Jesus was born, but it's much deeper than that and much simpler too.

As generations passed, Christmas became a day to bestow gifts upon loved ones. As the visitors to the manger brought gifts to the Lord Jesus, God on earth, we too mimic that event. As time went on, and never more so than now, the message of Christmas has been drowned in a sea of financial and material acquisitions. Everyone partakes in this convoluted celebration of Jesus's birth, and few acknowledge what exactly occurred so long ago.

The completeness we seek in this life will not come from material or financial gain. This illusion, created by your ego, will always lead you down a path of emptiness. Our true sense of completeness can only come through acknowledging, recognizing, and putting to use the event that took place with the birth of Jesus.

The gift that was given that day was to mankind from our Creator—God; it was a gift given to us during our separation from our Source—heaven. The gift is a simple gift but at the same time a mighty gift—a gift that could solve all the problems of this world and bring us to realization that love, true love, as God loves us, is the one and only religion. Without this gift, none of this is possible. The gift, in one word, is forgiveness.

Yes, Jesus came to teach us how to live, but most of all He was sent to forgive us our sins. Death on the cross was symbolic representation of the death of our sins. God also showed us that death is only an illusion, and true life occurs when we are one with God.

The key that opens the gates of heaven and the true joy and life that will be found in the light of God is forgiveness. This simple but mighty gift given to us by God through the birth of His Son is all but forgotten in the dash to material gain.

On this day especially, as with all days, offer your gift of forgiveness to others around you. The path to heaven is paved with forgiveness and leads to the true love of God—heaven.

If I had received only these two messages on December 24 and 25, I think my viewpoint of life would have changed drastically. Life, the three *r*'s as I refer to them - realization, recognition, revelation - and the true meaning of Christmas have never been so clear to me until now. Simple, to the point, and believable, these two messages alone could alter one's outlook, but more messages were to come. Deeper yet clearer, complex yet simple, the messages continued, and I hope they never stop.

CHAPTER 9
I AM ALWAYS WITH YOU, I AM IN YOU, AND I AM YOU

The first day of the New Year did not disappoint me in a couple of ways. Temperatures were extremely warm for New England, and the skies were crystal clear. Of course, a New Year's message came forth also.

January 1, 2012

    Your New Year has begun and brought forth a symbolic representation of how the rest of your life should proceed. Things are not as they seem. Your calendar says winter, yet the air is warm. Frost that has crept in during the darkness of night clings to the grass only to melt away in the light of a new beginning. The clarity of the sky allows the light of the sun to warm your face. This day has broken through the winter and feels as though it has come three months too soon.
    Today shows you that anything is possible; use this day as a reference for the rest of your life. The light, My light, will melt away the past. No longer can negative experiences cling to you in the warmth of My love. The clarity you see in this cloudless sky represents the clarity you can and must possess with regard to Me. I am the light; I am the all that you seek. Through My guidance your path is clear, is safe, is correct. Acknowledge Me and seek Me out on the darkest nights and cloudiest days. Only My light, through your faith, will be the beacon guiding you on the path of understanding. Clear your mind, as the sky of this new day in your New

Year is clear. Cast away the storms of negativity and the clouds of defeat that invade your mind.

Through this clarity of who you are and who I am, My light can burst forth in your life. Carry this light each and every day of your life, walk with me, and melt away the pain of your past. Follow this light, My light, to a bright and blessed future.

My light will shine through all events in your life, bringing forth the message you seek. There is no defeat in My light, no pain, no suffering, no torment; only peace, love, and a new awareness will shine forth.

As the sun still shines on cloudy days, rise up through the clouds and seek Me out. I am there; I have always been there. Your walk was never alone.

This was a perfect message for a perfect day. The love of winter is a distant memory for me. Spending all my life in New England, taking up skiing in elementary school, and traveling to my parents' vacation house in Maine just because there was fresh snow was fun, and the memories can never be lost. That being said, snow-covered trees under a clear blue sky, wood smoke wafting through the air, and the footprints of little creatures sneaking around in the snow at night is better left for a Christmas card. Yup, I've kind of had it with winter. Is it old age or the unpredictable weather in Connecticut that has turned me so cold to winter? One day snow, then a thaw, then rain, then ice, and then sun—this part of New England has a hard time deciding what winter should be. I have always said, "If we would just get snow, then I'll be happy." God answers all prayers, and the 2009–2010 winter was one for the record books. We had record-setting snow and no place to put it. It snowed in December, and it was still on the ground in April. As I am writing this now, the temperature is in the nineties, our central air is on the fritz, and I just walked by a giant snow blower I bought to combat the snow that never showed this winter. Thank you, God … well, except for the air-conditioning problem.

The next message is one that talks of forgiveness, a common thread among pretty much all the messages. God resides in each and every one of us, so that means the person who irritates you, makes you mad, or for that matter is your enemy also has God contained within him or her. It is our free will that guides us to be caring, helpful, and generous people. It is also free will that allows us to choose anger, hate, resentment, etc. Ultimately though, it is forgiveness of others and forgiveness of ourselves that is most important. The most difficult thing to do is to forgive someone for a wrong that has been committed against us, but it is the most important thing to do. Furthermore, the life each of us lives as a human is not really life at all; it is just a series of events to assess how far we have come on our spiritual walk. We must try to see God in each and every person we meet throughout our daily travels. Many times this is much easier said than done. The next message clarifies what I'm trying to say.

January 11, 2012

    First and foremost, remember forgiveness is the key to heaven's gate. I have bestowed this gift upon you countless times and will do it again countless more times. Life is a series of events you experience to better understand who you really are. Ultimately there is no right and wrong in the spiritual sense. The human existence is not life; it is purely an event comprised of events to help you recall who and what you truly are.

    I created you, a perfect representation of Me. So too I have created all others in My likeness. My light resides in each and every person. The light of My presence is carried in your soul, which for the present moment resides on this earthly plane.

    You have been sent here to remember above all that life never ends. You do not die, and I will not return. How can you rise from the dead when your soul already experiences everlasting life, and how can I return when I have never left? Remember, I reside in you and in every living being on the planet.

    With this understanding the inescapable importance to forgive is clear. When you don't forgive yourself, you don't forgive Me. You are saying to yourself, "I am less than perfect." How can this be? I created you, I live in you, I am you, and you are Me.

    When you can wrap your mind around this, your walk to enlightenment will truly begin. When you can see this in all others, you will be well on your way. At this point, no sin is too great to be forgiven, for the reality of this life and what occurs in it will be known to you. This life is not real life, the end-all, the ultimate existence.

True life, the life you seek, the life you're here to remember, is in the light of heaven—a light that shines within you, although shrouded by the fog of drama that you fall into on your earthly walk.

Your human condition causes you to seek this drama through what you watch, read, and are taught about how the world really is. The world is really nothing—nothing more than events for you to experience, to see for what they really are, and to forgive.

Every soul on this earthly walk carries the heavy burdens of past wrongs performed against them. The load, at times, can be unbearable because it is a load you carry alone. This burden can be removed by forgiveness, a Godly act of compassion and understanding for what truly is. An equal number of acts of kindness have been bestowed upon you, but you fail to carry those, those which are carried with the help of Me.

Your perception of good and bad in some cases has been twisted. To you—coming from the light—acts of kindness are to be expected, so you sometimes take for granted these gifts from the Divine. The so-called bad things that happen are different to you, incomprehensible at times, totally against who and what you are. These you choose to carry, these you give power, and these, because of your limited understanding of what is real and not real, are not viewed as the same type of gift.

There will come a time when you realize that every experience is a gift from Me. Perceived enemies in your life are sent to boost you up, to help you rise above, not to bring you down. Difficult personal times are not meant to break you but to bend you toward Me. Through all the good and the bad, I have never left you, or anyone else for that matter. When you can see Me in your enemy, you will see clearly.

Do not hide from these experiences, experiences you have gone through many times and many lives before. Realize that you have been the so-called good one and the bad one many times over, each time experiencing what was necessary for your spiritual evolvement. I have walked beside you each time, offering the gift of forgiveness.

To hide from this reality is to make you an island, albeit a deserted island, void of any life or awareness of the light of God. Be cautious not to fall into the false comfort of extended periods that "aloneness" may offer. Seek alone time for communication with self, which by default would be communication with Me. I am in you, I am you, and you are Me.

Your avoidance of situations or events because of a lack of self-gratification has two sides. Yes, take care of yourself, your spiritual self, by all means; by doing so you become a blessing to others. Instead of a deserted island, you become a place of safe harbor for those floundering in a sea of torment. An event, unfulfilling or unrewarding on your part, may have been a Godsend you participated in during another soul's journey, the same journey all walk side by side in. Do not forget My ways; they are least of all mysterious. And do not forget how I work. I work through you, I work through others, I work through friends, and I work through foes. The enlightenment comes when you realize you are not experiencing true life but getting glimpses of what true life really is: a not-too-distant memory of a place of peace, joy, and all knowing, a place where you see Me and see yourself for who you truly are.

This message shows that our perception of good and bad is a little off. In hindsight, every event or situation works for our Higher Good, and we must view this as such. We are concentrating on a human existence and forgetting that we are Spirit and what matters in this existence is what we have become through our experiences. Perceived as good or bad, right or wrong, it doesn't really matter on the physical level. Also, we must be careful in choosing what baggage to carry on our walk. How often has all the good you have done been forgotten because of the one time you were less than perfect? We all have experienced this wrong committed against us, but have we ever been on the other side of the equation?

The next message talks of seeing the good in every situation, and if you look closely enough, you'll find it. That's great for me to say when everything is going smoothly; the trick is to consistently acknowledge that the trials we are subject to are for a higher purpose. When I look back on my life, I see (and I'm sure you see this in your own situations) that what I perceived as negative at the time it was occurring proved to be positive down the road. The lost job presented a new opportunity; the financial failures taught me better spending habits, and the death of a loved one ended suffering. Yes, there are many situations that are almost impossible to comprehend as eventually being a positive, such as the unexpected death of a child or the taking of another's life. I in no way claim to have all the answers, and I struggle with seeing the good in some situations, but at some point in our spiritual journey these answers too will be revealed.

February 3, 2012

Blessed are those of you who still see the sun when clouds envelop your life. On even the most overcast days, the sun is still shining. The rains that pour forth are a necessary and nourishing event. All sun and no rain make a desert—a place on the surface devoid of life, unable to give back until the seasonal rains fall. Then even a barren, desolate wasteland springs to life. Seeds long forgotten sprout, bringing forth the bloom of wildflowers, whose beauty while short-lived is no less intense. There are those of you who seek to bask in the sun and just as many who look forward to the rains that permeate the soil to bring forth new life.

You must be the one to recognize and embrace both events on your planet. You must be the one to recognize and embrace both the rain, the cloudy days, and the bright sun-filled days in your life.

The clouds will and must come into your life. Just as on earth, the sun is shining right above the clouds. I too am with you on your cloudy days. The clouds will bring forth a cleansing—a nourishing of a soul, which would become parched and devoid of life if it were not for the experiences that this life brings. The events that you perceive to be negative are events that bring you recognition, realization, and the revelation of who you truly are.

These stormy events have no effect on you when you come to the realization that you are a Divine being, a soul created by and inhabited by Me, God. Realize that I made you, I am in you, and I am you. I am the light you seek on a cloudy day. I am with you, around you, and in others you meet. You can find Me in the brightest time of your life and the darkest. I have never left you; I never forget you. It is you who has forgotten; it is you who has lost the knowledge; it is you who needs to remember.

There are no positive or negative events in this life; there are just experiences—experiences to make you realize and acknowledge My presence in each and every one of you. I am ever present and everlasting. You too have everlasting life—not this life but a Divine life, true life. Your experience here on earth in this lifetime is to bring to you the recognition of this, to remember who and what you really are. The trials and tribulations you experience are the rains that wash away, that nourish, that bring forth new life in the form of a new awareness: I am always with you, I am in you, and I am you.

Blessed are those who see the sun through the clouds. Blessed are those who see Me in themselves and in others. Blessed are those who see and understand My ways.

I feel blessed that I have received such thought-provoking messages. With an open mind and a humbled heart, I share these thoughts with you.

The next message basically states that we are responsible for the events of this lifetime. We arrive here with specific goals to achieve, and we have created the events to reach those goals. We must remember that these events are not permanent, and the question of why can be found within ourselves. We must experience the negative to know the positive, and nothing in this life can destroy who and what we truly are. We are one with God, and God is one with us, so we are one with each other. It's a nice concept, but at the same time it's a little scary. Come on, admit it. You're tapping into your human side and asking, "I'm one with so-and-so?"

February 3, 2012

This path you call life has been chosen by you. Its ups and downs, twists and turns are all creations of your spirit—the purpose of which has been locked away in the recesses of your mind.

Every ship, every plane, before it embarks on a journey, has a destination. You also come here with a destination. Seeking a place of recognition, a place of realization, you spend a lifetime seeking the answer found at your final destination.

Forgetful of your Source, forgetful of who and what you truly are, you wander this path questioning, "Who am I? What's the point? When will it end?" Answers to all this and much more are found in you, your Higher Self—the you I have created, the you I reside in. I would not place you in a world of pain, suffering, and heartache. The world I create is of peace, love, and forgiveness—a life everlasting.

The events that you create are experiences that last a blink of an eye, that disappear like a snowflake in the sun, and that, like a snowflake, are never created exactly the same again.

These experiences are necessary for you to reach this final destination. You cannot feel love if you haven't felt hate; peace without anger; forgiveness without persecution; light without darkness. These experiences bring you closer to your destination. You start to realize the purpose of this life and begin to recognize who and what you are. You are a Divine being created by Me, and I am a part of you, thus you are a part of Me. The difference between us is that I know this and you cannot acknowledge the interconnectedness we possess. I have walked this earth in a human form. I have seen God in Myself and all others. I have recognized the interconnectedness we possess. I am in you, you are in Me, and I am in others, so we are all one. This awareness brings with it the ability to forgive, truly forgive. You forgive others, and in turn you forgive yourself. This forgiveness shines the light on your destination: true unconditional love.

This true and everlasting love is what opens the gates to heaven. The snapshot you call life will happen over and over, and I will continue to open the gates of heaven for you. There will come a day when you will possess the love needed to open the gate for others.

I am you, you are Me, and we are one.

The concept that we are one with God is easier to handle than the fact that we are one with each other, but that is the human physical side of me thinking out loud. Still, the messages I have received so far are easier to fathom than the fact that we live, die, and lie in wait to be resurrected.

The next message was undoubtedly sent for me. At times I questioned the validity of these messages, and at times I even thought they were a distraction in my daily life. Was I losing my mind or fantasizing, or was it a vivid imagination? Now I can absolutely say no to all of the above. Describing me to a tee, the following message hits home on all the doubts and questions that sought refuge in my mind. God has blessed us with an instruction manual to life and revealed most of the secrets to us. We must take comfort in the fact that God is with us every step of the way, and when we think he has left us behind, it is we who have forgotten about Him.

February 12, 2012

Here you sit again, compelled to write. The answers to your questions about where and from whom these words come seem to elude you. The answer you seek comes through trust and faith, a trust and faith that you already possess, a trust and faith that needs to be released fully as opposed to being bottled up and poured out drops at a time. The only control you possess in this life is to control your beliefs. Release the shackles created by your world that hold back the openness you have stored up inside. Cut away the chains of worry, envy, ego, resentment, anger, and control. Release yourself fully to Me. Allow my words to sink in, to be read, and to be shared.

You have and are being given an instruction manual to life, its purpose and its wonders. You have prided yourself in not needing to read instructions. You now have been given the task to write them.

The gift that you have been given by Me in this life, to assemble, repair, create, and understand the workings of this physical world, has served you well. This innate knowledge you possess is now overshadowing the purpose of your existence. Things and abilities of this world no longer will hold importance to you. Your path is going to change regardless. Your resistance to change is weakening.

Take comfort in the fact that I do not seek perfection in results, only perfection in effort. Do not resist the urge to read, to write, to openly express that which you receive. Find no guilt in your lacking when it comes to following these instructions.

The fact that you have read instructions on flying an airplane, playing a piano, using a computer, or even living your life does not mean you will be an instant success. So it is true with the messages you have and you will continue to receive. Only through practice, practice of trust in Me, practice of faith in Me, will you reach the goal—a goal that your spirit is driven toward, that it knows exists, that it can't be without, the goal of being completely open in trust and faith in Me, God, and the acknowledgment that I am in you and therefore with you every step of the way.

Therefore, once and for all, read the instructions you have written, write the instructions you are going to receive, and live your life by the words given to you through the Divine. Seek not the perfection required to follow these words but welcome the awareness of when you haven't. Through this exercise you will be reminded of who and what you are, a spiritual being experiencing a human existence. All the trials and tribulations of this life will gain a new perspective. Through this exercise you will acknowledge My presence, and you will feel My strength and My mercy pick you up.

The burdens and worries of this life will be cast off by you and carried by Me, and the gifts you receive are gifts from Me.

You have seen these words before: *follow these instructions*. This time follow them, write them, receive them, and share them. Life does come with instructions; you have been blessed to receive them.

Well, that sums things up quite well. Never one to read instructions for anything, I enjoy assembling, building, and figuring out how everything works together. This is not possible when it comes to what life is all about. We all have questioned the reason life is the way it is, and now I believe we are being told. We are being told how it works, why this or that happens, and above all that the life we live right now is not true life. I stress again that this is not coming from me but rather through me. So anyone who knows me as the imperfect person that I am, I'm still that person; only now, I'm aware of it.

CHAPTER 10
EXPERIENCE MY STRENGTH, NOT TO CARRY YOU BUT TO LOVE YOU

Wow is what went through my mind when I reread the next message. The following message hits home on what I think the big change for 2012 was. It was an end to this world as we know it, and a great awakening will begin on earth. At the very least, the world for me had changed markedly. There also is some clarification contained in the text, and our interconnectedness with each other is explained. God is making every effort to get this message across, and in my case, it hadn't fallen on deaf ears.

March 4, 2012

The awakening your planet seeks, needs, and must have is becoming obvious to you now. In your writings you once described life as a classroom. This is not entirely correct. The point being made in that comparison is not one of gaining knowledge as much as it is of gaining awareness.

You, and all life, have come here to experience an alternative existence on earth. This experience on earth does not change who or what you truly are; it merely gives you a different perspective from the one you previously possessed.

This journey you call life does not negate, neutralize, or remove the one quality all life possesses: Me. My presence and importance in your life cannot be changed, minimized, removed, overpowered, or destroyed. As the Creator, the Source, I am part of you, you are part of Me; we are one in spirit. This true life cannot be destroyed.

So your journey from the Source to this lifetime, as with all lifetimes, has been chosen by you. A journey mapped out specifically for you to gain a better view of the bigger picture.

As told to you before, your positive experiences have no value until you have something to compare that to—a negative experience. These negative experiences have no effect on a spiritual being, a divine being—that which you are. Your humanness is only a tool to facilitate the experience. Death, pain, turmoil are only illusions, and your acceptance of this fact is crucial.

I am the Source. I live in you and you in Me. The awareness of this has been forgotten in your human journey. The acceptance of this fact is imperative to the Great Awakening that is about to envelop your planet.

If you inhabit Me and I inhabit you and, as stated in the past, I inhabit all, then you are one with every person on the planet. This is not new knowledge for you; it is a reminder of what is. You, and everyone here, are here to remember who and what you are: one spiritual, Divine being that is one with God.

The human connectedness you possess in your family tree is no more powerful than the spiritual connectedness you possess with them, your neighbor, your enemy, or the soul residing in some far-off country. For that matter, the spiritual connection to those who have passed is no less a bond than the one you have with a spouse or child. As a matter of fact, the spiritual connection is much stronger than any genetic connection because I am present in this spiritual bond.

The awakening that this world must experience is the awakening to the fact that all of you are connected, are intertwined, are equal, are special, are inhabited by Me. Through My presence in each and every one of you and each and every one of you being one with Me, ultimately you are one with each other.

The awakening to this fact brings the awareness to you and to all who read these words that a change must come over your world. Through this Divine and unbreakable connection, your actions to and with others have an effect not just on them but the same effect on you. By exhibiting anger, you feel anger; by dismissing others, you dismiss yourself; by hurting others, you hurt yourself; by forgiving others, you forgive yourself; by loving others, you love yourself; and by performing any of these acts toward another, you perform them toward Me. *What you do to the least of you, you do to Me* is much easier to comprehend now, isn't it?

In short, you are part of Me, I am a part of you, they are part of Me, and I am a part of them. Therefore, they are a part of you, and you are a part of them. The awareness of this interconnectedness is what is needed now in your world. Through God all things are possible; therefore, through you all things are possible. Bring forth the recollection you possess of My presence to all you meet. They, in turn, will bring forth the awareness of My presence to others, and the word will be out. No longer hidden in the shadows of your private thoughts, my name—God—will be heard across the lands and through all peoples. My message will be heard, followed, and adhered to. The light of heaven will rain down upon the earth, and the light of knowledge will forever push away the darkness.

I ask again: how different would our lives be if we adopted the viewpoints revealed up to this point? I can't see how we could be negatively affected. I also question those who still can't have a belief in God or a higher power, the Divine, and everlasting life. Where then do these words in the messages come from? My own mind? I find it impossible to think so. Still, we will come across the naysayers who need to have some physical proof of a Divine presence. To them I say look around you and gain the awareness the messages speak of and see that some events are much more than coincidence. The next message attempts to change the perspective that life is just a series of coincidences.

March 10, 2012

The awareness of who and what you are must be acknowledged for the awakening to occur. Each and every one of you are made up of the same physical properties, but each and every one of you have differing goals, desires, and results.

The easiest way for you to comprehend this is with the comparison of two different vehicles. All made up of the same "ingredients," what makes one vehicle outperform another? Is it the shape, the paint, the outward appearance that makes it outperform another? Or is it what's inside, unseen by most when viewed from the showroom floor? The engine, the suspension, and the technology that was used in the production of that vehicle are what make it special. So too is it true for your human counterparts.

You've heard this many times before in many ways: it's what's inside, don't judge a book by its cover, etc. This thought process must be used when surrounding yourself with those who can bring out the best in you. Are the only souls that are good for you the ones that agree, flatter, and make your life easier? Or do you learn more from the ones that "push your buttons," challenge you, anger you, or even disgust you?

The latter of the two gives you an opportunity to rise above your comfort zone; that allows you to experience pain, anger, and compassion and exhibit goodwill. This group may be the most important in your spiritual evolvement.

The ocean viewed from the shore is a wondrous sight, but the real life is found below the surface. What the ocean is all about is below the waves. The winds whip up the waves, but down below, the life—the beauty of the deep—is unaffected.

All of you must view yourselves as an ocean. On the surface things may be rough, your physical body may be tormented, but inside your true life resides. The energy that is you, your soul, is impervious to the destruction of the physical.

In this way too all of you are the same, but the paths you have chosen are different. All leading back to Me, the paths chosen may be straight, haphazard, or even littered with negative experiences. All of this and more is necessary for your individual evolvement.

The awakening will occur for all of you; it is impossible for it not to. You are one with Me and I with you. The time frame for this event is different for each of you.

Bear in mind that I am the Creator of all. In My likeness you live, and in My light you will reside. The differences in the physical only serve to awaken the spiritual. The differences in the path all lead to the same place: Me. Chosen wisely, the journey of free will can be a lengthy one, but I am by your side each and every step, not to guide but to support. Seek Me out in all your decisions so as to experience My strength, not to carry you but to love you.

Once again the preceding message builds upon the previous one. Even though written days apart, all of these messages build upon each other. In the beginning, when receiving all of these messages, I thought to myself, *Nice, but what about ...?* Sooner or later my question was answered in a subsequent message. A few key words keep popping up over and over in the messages: *love, free will, awareness, forgiveness, spirit, eternal, everlasting, interconnectedness,* and *peace.* The two most important words, in my opinion, are *love* and *forgiveness*—two words that must go hand in hand, simple and yet complex. The mastery of both is paramount to evolution in the spiritual realm.

We live in a blessed country. Despite our political differences and the imperfect way our country deals with its neighbors at times, I challenge anyone to find a better place to live. I have met customers in my business who have come from the Middle East, Asia, Africa, Europe, Central and South America, and one thought is common among all: the United States is the greatest country in the world in which to live. Yes, I can hear many now going off about all that is wrong with our political system, justice system, social programs, etc., but for the moment, concentrate on the good qualities our country possesses.

In the next message, we are given a glimpse of why this country is the desired land and why it has been blessed by the hand of God. Unfortunately God's influence is lost in our quest to maintain our quality of life and is all but forgotten.

March 11, 2012

The awakening your planet seeks is near at hand. It must be. It will be. When it occurs is up to you and those around you. All possess the knowledge, the vision, and the desire when the connection to God is unbroken.

Your country, the United States, has been blessed. The blessing came with the few who sought out a land of freedom, freedom to worship their God when and how they chose, and a land where all men were created equal. Those two things alone were enough to ensure God's grace upon your land for eternity. Were these ideals put into practice? Does your country still strive for those ideals, or are words enough to satisfy the masses?

God expects perfection in efforts, not results. His lack of control over your free will is an example of this. At any moment He could instill His power over anyone or any place, but He needs you to seek Him out for His blessing to be realized.

The first battles fought in the new land were for freedom (freedom of worship), for the pursuit of happiness, and to acknowledge that all men are created equal and should not be under the power of any one person. All subsequent wars were fought on the same premise, but were and are you being truthful with yourselves? The riches of this world are for the benefit of all, not just for those who reside where they are found. The exchange of the world's resources must be distributed not for one country's benefit but must be used in a way that all can benefit. Battles rage now over resources. Woe to those of you who possess no such resources on your land; you are forgotten by the powerful of your world, for they seek what you cannot offer.

This is not the plan God had for this world, your country, or the souls residing here. The blessings bestowed upon your country were granted when your path and ideals were that of God's. In the past hundred years alone the inventions of the great minds in your country—electricity, communication, transportation, medicine, etc.—were all designed to bring people closer. Foods from far-off lands, information from other cultures, and cures for diseases could be spread across the globe. People helping people for the betterment of all, God's plan—it has not been adhered to.

Your land, your planet, is on a collision course with greed and ego. The purpose of this life is to evolve. Evolve to a place of awareness of who and what you truly are. Enough messages have been given about that; now there are the chosen among you who must spread the awareness.

Your own ego struggles with the apparent liberalness of all this thinking. You have spent your life working for what you have; everyone should earn what they receive. Do you think your efforts have not been blessed by God? That your position in life is all of your own making? How dare you after all you have written.

Instead, your conservative viewpoint is right on the mark with God's. Help those who are truly in need, show off the blessings God has given you in life, and be sure to acknowledge them as such. Use your gifts in a way that can benefit others. Was it not God who said, "Teach a man to fish …"?

Your country has failed to do this; your world has failed to do this, and this has nothing to do with a political ideology. It is an obvious observation.

Yes, there are those who need aid, support, and provision, and the wealth of your country should be used for this. Unfortunately, it has been perverted into a way that those who have can control those who don't, and it keeps the evolvement process at bay.

Your society is not evolving; it is gravitating toward the negative. Why is that? Why are bad habits copied? Why are negative behaviors interesting in your world? Free will and the lack of awareness of your connectedness to God is the reason.

Acts of free will, when entwined with God's vision and blessing, serve to better all mankind. A perfect example is the development of technologies you possess today, and their intended benefit to all. Instead, they have served to separate the haves from the have-nots even more.

Your people must devise a way to reconnect with the purpose of your Founding Fathers. Ego must be erased from the equation. Seek a world that benefits all. That doesn't mean everyone has exactly the same things, the same desires, the same results. It would be a world where everyone and their choices are choices that are for the benefit of all.

The country where you reside started out on the right path, but it has strayed. God has become a word only spoken in a select group of buildings where His vision, His wisdom, and His forgiveness remain trapped.

Seek out His vision and His wisdom, and ask for His forgiveness. He has followed you down the wrong path, patiently waiting for you to see, for you to acknowledge, for you to wake up to the fact that you have strayed. Before you ask, you have been forgiven; before you redirect your path, He sees you putting your best foot forward; and before you admit to needing His help, He offers His hand.

He knows the path. Freely reach out to Him and follow, lead others, and reach the destination your soul seeks.

Well, that pretty much sums up what our country has become. We are a nation that tries to provide materially to everyone instead of requiring everyone who can to pick up their end of the log. Of course, there are those who have genuine needs, but at the same time there are people looking for a free ride, and those in power are willing to give it to them to stay in power. I am not trying to make God's messages a political statement; instead, if we look at things with the open-mindedness this book requires, it is quite evident where we have strayed as a country. Our policies, laws, and actions do not always serve to benefit the majority in our world.

Waking up to the first sentence in the next message one morning in March was not that surprising. I had been getting used to waking up to phrases or words that developed into messages; only this time, I pulled up the shade, and the physical world was shrouded in fog.

March 14, 2012

Your life is the fog through which you try to see. Rise above the clouds, and the vision as to who and what you are becomes clear.

Your hurts, your pains, your inadequacies are not what define you but are your catalysts to evolve, to rise above, to forgive.

Above the clouds the expanse of clarity is endless. Rise above your life; enter into the state of knowledge of who and what you are.

Forever more you shall view yourself as a Divine being, one with God. The life you have led and will lead is merely a tool—a vehicle for your ascension to higher awareness.

Take heed of these messages; they come not from a place where you reside but from a place you have come from and a place you shall return.

Rise above the fog, the clouds, and your world and embrace the newfound knowledge you possess. The message is clear; it is you and you alone who must see through the fog.

Basically this short message was telling me, telling us, that it is our own perception that keeps us from seeing and experiencing who and what we really are. Everything we experience is intended to bring us to a greater awareness of the Divine connection we have with God. We must see this connection despite what is going on around us, and even if we don't see it at the moment does not mean it's not there.

The following message reinforces the idea that each of us has a very specific path to follow in this life. This path and its obstacles were chosen by you to bring you to a greater awareness. We must be vigilant to follow our chosen path, and we should seek out the guidance afforded us by our connection with God.

March 25, 2012

The path you stand before is littered with challenges. Your continuation of this journey must be evaluated by you, and only in conjunction with God's plan can a determination be had.

Is your path the start of something positive, a healing or a benefit to others? To embark on such a journey to the positive, the negative must be experienced; the obstacles before you were purposely placed. Ask yourself, "Do they come from me to excuse my failure, or do they come from God to redirect?"

Do not seek the answer from outside but rather from within. God is an everlasting presence inside you, and His guidance will allow you to receive the right answer. The answer does not elude you; you avoid the acknowledgment of receiving it.

Pray:

"Lord, grant me the vision to see the path before me, the wisdom to take it, and the faith in knowing You are by my side. Take my hand in yours and lead me to where I must go to serve You. Pull me over the obstacles that block my path, chosen by me through You. Carry me when I fail, and infuse Your strength in me to persevere. The path I seek is service to You. Thank you for the gifts given to me to achieve this purpose. Thank you for those who recognize my gifts, and thank you for those whose lives I touch as a conduit for Your healing power.

Forgive my moments of doubt, my questioning, and my lack of stamina. I receive my strength through You to continue on the path of light You have set before me. Through You and with You, my journey is complete. I accept and receive Your love to hold and to share."

This prayer introduces, once again, our need for faith—faith in God and faith in ourselves. It reminds us again that our walk is ours alone, but we do not take it alone.

Chapter 11
Seek God's Perspective

Fear has no place in a spiritual being, and the next message sets this straight. Reminding us that He is always in our lives, God questions why we still at times don't acknowledge Him. We still fail to see His work in our lives, and jokingly He reminds us that through Him we succeed. Through my awareness of God in my life, I can and should make others aware of His presence in their lives. Through this awareness, fear will be dispelled, and the world will develop into a place where another's position is taken into account in every decision.

The world is going through a trying time, and it is our collective responsibility to correct this situation. Those of faith and those who possess this greater awareness are going to be responsible for spreading the word. God is real, we are one with Him, and life is everlasting.

April 4, 2012

The fears you harbor in this life are yours alone to conquer. Imaginary yet real, singular yet many, the fear you possess is created solely by you through your lack of awareness. Haven't you heard enough already to realize? Haven't you seen enough to recognize? Haven't you been through enough to acknowledge the presence of Me in your life? Still you gravitate toward anything that can perpetuate your continued walk in fear. This must be conquered by you alone. I do not forsake you, but this is yours alone. Created by you and those around you, it must be destroyed by the same.

You have written, you have read, and you must share the revelations contained in the messages received. Have you no recollection of an event or situation that you went into with fear and trepidation only to emerge and say, "That wasn't so bad; I did pretty well"? I accept your belated thanks.

You see, I am with you every step and every moment of your life. Ever present, I am in you and available to you for guidance, but you must seek it. The guidance, the strength, the wisdom is yours to tap into. Many times before I have told you how I operate, how this whole human experience unfolds, and how to find peace and understanding.

Your awareness is awakening. Now awaken others. Ah, I sense your fear—needless fear. I have given and will continue to give you the tools necessary to achieve. You are my conduit for this specific task, just as others have been my conduits for healing, teaching, guiding, and saving.

As you and those around you gain this awareness, you will begin to see the beauty of this life and the world you live in. Not a perfect place but a place of potential to be perfect, your world is suffering because of a lack of awareness, fear.

Peoples have fought peoples, countries have robbed countries, individuals have destroyed individuals, and people have destroyed themselves all because of fear. They have what I need; they have what I want; and so on. The world has become a place of self-preservation. Get it before they do, get them before they get us—the world has turned into a chaotic tit for tat.

Who was forgotten in all of this? Whose message fell on deaf ears? Even those who claimed to know Me went against My word. I am the forgotten one. My name is not allowed in many places, people hesitate to say My name, and institutions of higher learning even try to teach of My nonexistence.

Then when tragedy befalls your planet, there are those of you who ask, "Where was God …?" I'm right here in each and every one of you. I am in the innocent child, and I am in the terrorist who can destroy so much. I am present in all but powerless in many—powerless to control the free will I give to you as a gift to propel your evolvement. The same free will that guides those who run into burning buildings to save others is the same free will that drives those who kill. One is guided by the compass of higher good; the other guided by ego and self-serving ambitions.

Those who possess the compass of higher good are those more evolved spiritually and closer to Me, although they are no more loved. Yes, I did say that, and it is true. I have said before that I would not choose which of my children to destroy or condemn, just as you could not love one of your children more than another, but you could deplore an act committed by them.

The negative experiences of your world, although disappointing to Me, have no effect on Me. More so, they define who you have become. They show the path chosen by you and magnify the missed opportunities that existed when My path was not followed.

This world can teach you so much, and many societies, long forgotten, have mastered the earth's lessons. Nature takes care of itself, and all events in nature ultimately have a beneficial effect on all other aspects of nature. The circle of life that the Disney movie professed is really quite evident.

When humans sought to control the earth's resources, its peoples, and its events all for the sake of self-benefit, problems started. Your awareness of My presence will bring you to one logical and inescapable conclusion: every decision you make should be made with the emphasis on how it positively affects another person. That's all. If every choice made by countries, states, cities, and peoples was based on what common good would come, your world would survive in the way I intended.

The dreaded end of the world will not come by My hand but by yours. You are doing this quite well by yourselves. A new path must be forged, new ideas must be developed, and above all, a new awareness must be accepted. Have no fear; give yourselves back to Me. Let Me be your guide on the path to enlightenment. Although before I said it really doesn't matter, your choice will speak volumes as to what you have become.

The purpose of this life, as I have said before, is for your evolvement, your spiritual awakening, your recalling of who and what you are. You have always been, and will always be, a divine part of Me and I a part of you. So now, where is the fear? Where is the worry? Where is the confusion? The burden has now been lifted; you are lighter, and you are more aware.

I know there is one more seemingly insurmountable fear that I have not addressed. It is a fear that humankind has been tormented with forever. It too comes from a lack of understanding and the inability of you to accept who and what you are. It was not created as a negative experience, but it has developed into one by your own misconceptions. It is perpetuated by some societies, some of the most advanced societies, as an end to something and not a continuation, which it really is. It is what I call a welcome home. It is what you call death.

Stop. There is no death. Over and over I have said this, and still you walk in fear to the threshold of everlasting life. Accept Me, accept who and what you are, and open the door that you call death. Walk through as those before you have and experience the most glorious welcome home you have ever experienced. For your true home exists with Me and the unconditional love that abounds in heaven. You have returned from your "tour of duty" on earth safe and whole in your communion with Me, God.

Well, no one message really pales to another, but if there was only going to be one message, it would be this particular one. It mentioned all the points we must master in this life, from awareness to the ultimate—our view of death. No stone was left unturned in the explanation and clarification of our fears, the fears that ultimately hold us back from our true relationship with God.

As Easter approached, once again I received a holiday message with a little bit of a new twist on things. I feel that God himself woke me up to give me a message about Easter. It's getting easier saying that God has spoken directly to me, and I realize how that must sound. Where could these messages originate, and why would God speak to me or anyone else for that matter? This is the problem we as souls are having. Does it seem logical to have God in your life, God guiding you, or God providing for you and it not possible to communicate with Him? We are taught from a very early age that we must pray to God, and we should, but most importantly, we should talk to Him and listen to His response. I went through a period of my life when I prayed to God and then went to sleep without waiting for His response. Well, evidently He's gotten tired of that, and He wakes me up to give me a message. I guess His patience wore thin.

Well, God is making a point to tell us that He is with us every day and has never left our sides. We need to awaken to this fact and realize what the resurrection was really demonstrating to us.

April 8, 2012

Easter represents the resurrection of the Lord Jesus, a miracle unsurpassed since its occurrence. Or does it still continue today?

I resurrected in body and soul as an example to all as to what is in store. All who pass from their human existence rise again as I have. Their souls release the clutch they once had on their bodies.

For generations, bodies have been prepared for burial, and loved ones put them to rest with the hope of rising again. There is no need for hope. The body placed in the ground will not rise. Why should it? It is your soul that rises to Me. In death you finally awaken to what you truly are.

I resurrected in body only as a tangible proof for the masses to get the message that life never ends. This event has been twisted into you dying and lying in wait for My return to rise and walk again. How is it that I can return when I have never left? That would truly be a miracle.

Time and time again I have tried to make you and others aware that I am part of you and you a part of Me. There will be a great awakening among you as to the validity of this concept. The true message that life never ends does not require the waiting and preparation for the so-called Second Coming.

Once again your spiritual existence, the true example of what you are, occurs simultaneously with your human existence. The awareness of this is pivotal in the awakening of your planet. Death is a non-event; it doesn't exist. It is merely a change in the events of your everlasting spiritual life.

A tree sheds its leaves in the fall; has the tree died? Flowers wither away; do they really die? A body fails to function; is that death? No. The tree is preparing for a new season, the flower either blooms again or drops seeds to sprout in spring, and the short event of your human existence awakens you to the glory of what is really occurring.

Your loved ones who have passed are aware of this. They reach out to you from what you perceive to be a distant place, but blessed are those of you who acknowledge the interconnectedness of the life you're living and the Divine.

No more do you see it as a separation, just as you are not separate from your family when you are separated by work or travel. Neither are you separated from Me or your loved ones who have graduated from this human experience.

Through you and others like you, a new awareness will and must be spread. Fear not the doubters you encounter. They may not receive the message now, but eventually they too will gain the awareness.

So do not wait for My Second Coming, for I have never left. Do not wait in fear for My wrath; it will never come. What there will be is an awakening, a realization, a revelation as to who and what you are, who and what you've become, and the newfound knowledge of how life really operates.

Many are dying for this information; you have received it long before your graduation. Take this blessing and make it known to others so that the life-changing events can unfold.

This message gives us information that normally wouldn't be available to us until we pass. We should view this as a gift. There may be some people among you who read this and say, "Oh, of course this is how it is." I can only reread these messages and say, "Wow! This is how it is!" This is a whole new perspective for me.

The next message speaks of our path, where it will take us, and who we will meet along the way. The people we meet may be lifelong partners or just passing acquaintances, but they all serve a purpose.

April 14, 2012

You now know the path you have chosen is yours alone. The realization that you are no longer beholden to the ways of others is clear. The path you walk is toward your Higher Good. Seek comfort in the fact that you are gently being guided, being protected, and being made aware of the changes you must make.

Your chosen path will and must intersect with the paths chosen by others. At times a quick acknowledgment is all there is; at other times it will be a walk side by side for a lifetime.

How do you choose when and if you should follow, lead, or leave the path you're on? Should you keep step with others on the same path?

Look inside; seek the answer from within. Is this meeting going to bring you to higher awareness, a realization, a validation of your spiritual self, or is it going to stifle and detract from this lifetime's evolvement?

The answer you seek will come to those with the awareness and acknowledgment of the ways of the Divine, for the path chosen by you is never truly walked alone. A guiding hand is always outstretched to you from others who have walked a similar path before. Your guides have reached out to you in the past and in the present, for they know the choice you've made, they know the destination you seek, and they know of the strength you need to succeed.

Forgotten are the ways of the universe that have been constant. The reminder of who and what we are must be heard and will be heard. The place you seek is the place from which you came. The place from which you came will be the place to which you return. The memories of who and what we are will be realized, and those of you who reach this realization in this lifetime will be the guides for others.

Reach out to those now who do not contain this newfound knowledge and bring others on your path to enlightenment.

Many times we have a "gut feeling" when we meet someone or are presented with a certain situation. This "gut feeling" is something we should pay attention to because it may very well be from one of our guides.

Forgiveness and how it is granted is the message in the next passage. Although it is the most important thing we should strive for on our path of spiritual evolution, forgiveness may be the most difficult to master. Unconditional forgiveness is the key to unconditional love, and one cannot occur without the other. I know it must seem impossible at times to grant someone forgiveness for a misdeed, and far be it for me to preach to anyone on this subject. We are all guilty of holding grudges, resentment, and hurt for spoken words or misdeeds against us, but the fact remains that we must somehow figure out how to forgive.

We've all carried the burden, the pain, and the negative thoughts associated with not being forgiving. Many times the people we are holding all these negative feelings toward are clueless to our suffering. They go about their lives seemingly unaffected by what is going on, and we carry this burden throughout our lives. We must forgive, stand in our truth, and acknowledge our position in the event requiring forgiveness. Quite possibly we had no part in the event and are truly innocent, but forgiveness is the key that opens heaven's gate. It may be one of the most difficult keys for us to utilize.

April 16, 2012

It has been said that forgiveness is the key that opens heaven's gate, but what is forgiveness, and how and when should it be granted?

The forgiveness discussed here is not the forgiveness granted to a child for an indiscretion. No less important though, the act of forgiveness that must be mastered is the forgiveness granted when a life-changing event is the end result of another's misdeed.

Forgiveness does not require that you forget; it only requires that you no longer carry. Forgiveness does not mean life does not change; it means you have gained acceptance for the new life that may result. Forgiveness does not mean there is no consequence for the misdeed, and the consequence should not be sought out of revenge.

This message was prompted by your thoughts of what is right and wrong in the actions of those close to you during recent events. The clarity you seek can be used in any situation and not just for those you pray for at the moment.

One of the most common forgiveness situations is the forgiveness that must be granted in personal relationships such as marriage. Forgive and forget is not exactly how it works, for that would impede the overall evolvement spiritually for all involved. Instead it means to offer forgiveness, accept what has occurred, and no longer carry it forward in your life.

First and foremost, you must learn to forgive yourself for the part you played in the event. No longer do you shackle yourself to the chains of guilt that hold you back on your walk in this life. The person who goes back over and over or tolerates again and again the negative behavior of a spouse is not practicing forgiveness. He or she is demonstrating a lack of awareness of what lesson needs to be taken from this event.

So too is it true for the perpetrator; many times the acceptance of a negative behavior by one spouse to another will continue, and a lesson would be lost were it not for a consequence.

In a situation where there is abuse, be it physical or emotional or the abuse of alcohol, forgiveness does not require the nonabuser to accept the negative events and carry on as if nothing has happened. The term *nonabuser* is used to show that both in this situation are victims. One is a victim of negative tendencies brought on by mental, emotional, societal, or physical effects on their lives, and the other—the more obvious—is the one on the receiving end of all this negativity.

Many times you will hear of spouses who have forgiven and taken back a spouse, and life goes on. Other times marriages dissolve, and each spouse goes on his or her separate way. One situation in the eyes of God is no different than the other.

Forgiving a spouse for a misdeed is releasing them also from the chains of guilt that bind them to an event or events. Do not seek vengeance or revenge; neither has a place in true forgiveness. Should you choose to pursue a life without the offending spouse, make that choice and make it with the awareness of what is best for your Higher Good. In many cases your walk without your spouse will be the catalyst for him or her to make the changes he or she needs to make in his or her life. Sometimes acceptance of negative behaviors and continuing with life as it was is just perpetuating the negative behaviors.

Seek out God in your decision. The answer lies within you as God resides within you. In all situations of forgiveness both parties are part and parcel of God—a fact that cannot be dismissed in our view of others.

Seek God's perspective. Would he want me to continue on this path, or is He guiding me elsewhere? Does He want my spouse to continue on the same path? Would God forgive with no strings attached? The answer is quite clear when not obstructed by society's beliefs and expectations.

You and God alone make these decisions. You and God alone choose your path, and you and God alone can forgive—starting with yourself.

Total forgiveness does not require the restoration of a relationship.

I know what some may be thinking, and I'm thinking the same as I read this message again. Forgiveness is very easy to do or say when an unspeakable wrong has not been committed against a loved one, spouse, or child you know. We think surely God must see all we do; he has to look down in judgment on the acts committed by some. But according to the messages I have received, He holds no judgment, and neither should we.

That's a tough one to swallow, but if we look at it another way, it becomes somewhat easier to understand. This life we are living on earth is not truly life at all. It is a collection of experiences for us to react to, and the reaction we display will show how far we have evolved spiritually. True life cannot be destroyed, and it occurs in heaven in relationship with God. There are those among us who view life on earth as purely an illusion, just a collection of events to assess how far we have come as spiritual beings. With that being said, any one event—be it miraculous or tragic, happy or sad, good or bad—is equal in significance if the realization that we are spirit, one with God, and enjoy everlasting life is kept first and foremost in our minds. None of this is saying that we wander around life with no care for tomorrow or what happens to us or those around us. But everything does matter with regard to how we interact with each other. We must display concern, empathy, compassion, love, understanding, and usefulness, and above all, we must practice forgiveness. That is where I'm at right now: practicing forgiveness. Who knows; I may master it in this lifetime.

The next message starts by describing exactly how I think and view our physical world. I have always had a desire to work with my hands, be it woodworking or in my present trade as a mechanic. I have always prided myself in figuring out how something works and what it would take to fix it. I find our mechanical world, and even the forces that shape our earth, fascinating. Now I have crossed over to a world that I and probably many others have wondered about. Why are we here, what happens when we pass, and how do we get from point A to point B?

The following message, along with others, addresses this curiosity and provides some insight into what is going on in the world we presently inhabit.

April 18, 2012

You have questions. Ask them. You seek answers. Listen for them. You've been given gifts. Open them. Each and every one of you has the connection to Me; use it, develop it, strengthen it. This can only be done through awareness.

You, specifically, see the world as some others do not. You cross a bridge; you look at what supports it. You drive on a road; you imagine the foundation below. You see a tree; you picture the roots that steady the giant. How things work in the physical and natural world intrigues you. You have now begun to look deeper, deeper into the world of the Divine.

You look at machinery and find interest not in what it does but how it does it. So too you now look at life. Birth, life, death—okay, that's what we experience, but how does it work and why does it occur are questions you are beginning to answer. You have found a place to receive these answers; it is the same place where all answers can be found: within.

The answers to all questions for all peoples reside within you. Tap into this well of knowledge that everyone possesses. The waters drawn up from a well aren't just sitting there; the water originated from the clouds, permeated the ground, and traveled for miles in underground aquifers to the point where it rises again out of the well.

So it is with all life; starting somewhere else, it travels only to rise again back from where it came.

The answers you seek are no less different. Contained in you, these answers come from somewhere else, from someone else.

You accept that there is a spiritual world around you, unseen by most but nonetheless still there. Like the grains of sand that make up glass, spirit surrounds you, invisible to most but right before your eyes.

Spirits, guides, angels, and other Divine beings infuse the answers you seek into your soul. You ask your question, but do you listen for the answer? You cannot hear us over the chaos that life on earth has become. Welcome the silence that enters your life, for then you will hear. Welcome the solitude you experience at times, for then you will be in the company of angels.

Any and all questions should be asked. Any and all desires can be fulfilled. All knowing is yours with the connection you have forged, so strengthen it, use it, and share it.

Share it, yes, but first take care of yourself. Seek what your heart and soul desires, not in selfishness but in selflessness. Through your gain, others will be helped; others will see the benefit of your awareness. Carry on with what is best for you so you may be a reservoir of strength and support for others. At times your dam must be closed; if not, the reservoir will run dry. There will be nothing left for you.

Be mindful of the alone time you spend restoring your reserves. This is not a selfish act but a selfless act. Through this restoration of energy, spirit, and body you can continue what I have sent you to do.

How do I do this? When do I have the time? I know the questions before you asked. I had the answer before you had the questions.

So you have asked. Now listen.

At first glance, many of the messages contained in this book would be considered rather far-out by some people. Others will read them and say, "Of course. This is the way it is." I was one of the people who would have said they were a little out there. Really though, who wouldn't? You are brought up with a particular belief system; it's all you know, and many of us don't like change. I for one would have probably gone the way of the dinosaurs if it were not for my wife, daughters, and the many special people we met along the healing path we were forced to take … well, we were guided on.

The messages I have shared have been met with all sorts of reactions. I seek feedback from those I share the messages with not to bolster my ego but instead to validate what I'm feeling and receiving. Gone are the doubts, the questioning, and the wondering about what is going on. I have succumbed to the fact and fully embraced the notion that a higher power and even *the* Higher Power is communicating with me. I am convinced also that we all receive messages in our lives, but we are too distracted to pay attention. Those times in your life when a loved one who has passed pops into your head or a familiar scent arises or a dream takes over your sleep are the times that Spirit is trying to get your attention.

The following message speaks to the fact that there are still people around me who are not ready to embrace the ideals presented in the messages I have received, and that is understandable. Society, religion, and ancestral upbringing are very powerful forces that work against the awareness we must seek. Only through openness and understanding can the real truth about God and His ways be realized.

April 23, 2012

You now are beginning to realize you reside in a realm of spiritual cluelessness. It is not that your counterparts lack any human intelligence; more so, they lack an awareness that you and some around you have begun to accept.

The words brought forth through the messages you have received are only new to you and others in this lifetime. Long forgotten are My words and our interconnectedness. Buried deep inside your soul, the answers you seek can be found. Each and every one of you came here with a knowing, a knowing that becomes stifled in your human evolvement. Many times this has happened, and for some it will happen many more times. A blessing of awareness has been bestowed upon you, and with it comes an obligation to share it. With this will come admiration and scorn, not for you but for the message. This has always been so and will continue, but fear not those who are not yet receptive to the message.

You are going to realize that conformity is not the answer in this existence. Conformity to people's rules, societal rules, and religious rules are not what I seek from you. What I seek is your acceptance and awareness in the one true "religion," if you will. It is love, unconditional true love, which can only be achieved through unconditional forgiveness. Master forgiveness, and the path will be clear.

Theologians and religious leaders for thousands of years have sought to explain and rationalize how I act and what I do. They have succeeded in only creating confusion—one religious group against another, one belief against another, and one group controlling another. All religions, regardless of intention, are rooted in ego: one group right, one wrong; one group chosen, one condemned. Families have been broken apart, lives ruined, and lives lost in My name and under the guise of religious beliefs.

You are starting to realize in your human existence that less is more and that simpler is better. So too is it true for your spiritual life. Your spiritual existence is about as simple as it can get. You are spirit, there is no death, and you and I are one. So in turn you have the knowledge of the Divine.

I have not created the complexities that hinder you; you have. I have not created the rules and regulations by which you live; you have. And I have not put distance between you and Me; you have. You have the responsibility for the path you choose; I have the responsibility to follow. I light many paths for you, and you must choose. One is not right or wrong; one is just better to serve your needs. Choose what brings you closer to Me. The choice is simple, and the answer is found in My questions: Are you serving yourself selfishly or selflessly? Are you answering to a Higher calling? Are you succumbing to societal rules? Are you holding back out of false loyalties to others' beliefs or wishes?

When you keep your spiritual self and the goals Spirit seeks in mind, the simplicity of the choice is quite evident. The simplicity of My message too is quite obvious: love one another unconditionally and practice true forgiveness. That's all. Imagine a world that can put this into practice. The difficulty lies within each and every person on the planet whose choice is ego-based as opposed to spirit-based. No longer would one have control over another; no longer would there be the haves and have-nots; and no longer would the acquisition of "things" be important. A far different world than you could possibly imagine would exist, but it is the world from which you came.

The journey here is not one of perfection but one of perspective. The negative needs to be experienced to know the positive, the complexities to appreciate the simplicities. You have been given the gift of awareness; you have been put in touch with like-minded people all in an effort to light your path.

Do not complicate matters. Do not overthink. Do not question that which you receive. So far you have kept yourself out of the messages, but do not keep the messages out of you. Be open, be receptive, and be generous in your sharing of these words.

The peace your planet seeks and the change that it is about to experience will come through two simple words: forgiveness and love.

This message, as with many, speaks of our ability to make a choice. We can choose to be sad, angry, resentful, bitter, happy, joyful, forgiving, peaceful, or caring. Also, I must not interject my opinions or thoughts into the messages received—something that I have been able to do. The meaning of the messages is not clear to me until I read them over. In addition to the choices offered to us, we must examine our perspective. How do we look at this or that? Do we only see the negative? Are we not seeing the bigger picture? No one can speak for me, and neither can I speak for anyone else about perspective. It is a compilation of past experiences and present conditions that create the prism through which we see the world, and it is not unalterable. Imagine that life is like looking out a series of windows. If you don't like what you see, pick another window. Once again, it's all about choice.

The following message addresses our need to receive as well as to give. Many of us have no problem giving help to a neighbor, friend, or family member, but we have difficulty accepting help offered to us. That's me; I'll help anyone but usually go it alone on projects I'm involved with. Well, that's not the way it is supposed to be. By not accepting help from others, we prevent others from receiving the fulfillment granted by offering and giving assistance to us. We are all one in an intertwined walk of evolvement.

April 24, 2012

Could a well continue to give life-giving waters if those waters were not replenished? Could a redwood stand were it not for the soil around its roots? Could your planet exist without the interconnectedness of life forms and natural events that occur on a daily basis? Why then do you feel you must and can go it alone on your walk through life?

Every aspect of the world, the universe, is intertwined to serve the other. All creation is reliant on other forces, comingled to create a great event.

So too is it true for you. Placed here to remember your spiritual connections and your connection to Me, you are designed with the natural instinct to help. Help is what some of you do too well at times.

The aid that others seek from you on their paths and the aid that some of you so readily dispense must be tempered. For like the well that continually gives up its life-giving waters, without replenishment it will cease to function.

You are no more than the least and no less than the greatest. In My eyes you are all the same—beings of light on a journey of awareness. Each and every one of you is intertwined like a spider's web—lives touching lives, action and reaction. Not one of you can take this walk alone. The reliance on each other is Divinely planned.

The blessing that you give others through support, through prayer, and through action brings you a sense of peace and fulfillment. So too must you receive. You can't give all of your energy to others without losing what you need for yourself. You must create time, a place, an activity that replenishes your reserves so you can continue to be the blessing that you are. Allow Me to be the source of your strength.

It is said that it is better to give than to receive, but more precisely, to give you must receive. Do not hold back in receiving help from others during your walk in life. As with the fulfillment you feel in serving others, so too do others seek that fulfillment in serving you. Graciously accept offers of aid from others. Nothing in the universe can stand solely on its own. Be open to the idea that no matter what side of the fence you stand, giving or receiving, you are still being a help.

By giving, it is obvious. But by receiving, you are helping another to receive the blessings of peace, joy, and purpose through which he or she can reach fulfillment.

There are two things, though, that must be given freely and without reserve. They are gifts from Me to be given to each other, gifts that are energizing and self-serving. The more you give, the more you receive.

Forgiveness and love—two gifts from Me to you with unlimited energy and in infinite supply. When forgiving others, you forgive yourself, and to love another, you must love yourself.

Keeping in mind the interconnectedness that we possess—I am in you, you are in Me, I am in everyone, so you are part of each other—the gifts of forgiveness and love, when freely bestowed upon others, are ultimately reflected back to you.

At this point in the writing of this book, I took a long break, a very long break. I constantly got the feeling as I reread these messages that people had to hear them. I had to write the book, and

I wished it was completed. Still I dragged on, not being able to get totally into the composition of this book.

So I planned a weekend by myself to kick-start the writing I had been avoiding so far. This weekend consisted of camping on the shores of Lake Winnipesaukee, fishing from my canoe, and of course, taking a big bite out of this book. Well, we all know the best laid plans many times fail.

My drive up was uneventful. I found a good site at the campground, and it was pretty quiet because it was the end of the season. I set up camp and enjoyed a great dinner for myself, alone in the beautiful woods of New Hampshire, and planned my next few days. The next day I planned to get up early, drop the canoe at the lake, and take a ride to my parent's house in Maine to snoop around. After that I planned on coming back, fishing until dinnertime, and enjoying a campfire. How difficult could this all be, and was I really asking for a lot? The Indian spirits that resided in those woods had another plan.

I woke up at 6:00 a.m. to a pretty steady rain and was like, *Come on. There was no rain in the forecast!* It stopped by 8:00 a.m., so I was still on. As I left for Maine, I realized that the site I was on was at the top of a pretty steep hill and that getting the canoe down to the lake, where of course there was no parking, would be quite a challenge. Getting it back up would be quite another thing. This was my first sign that my plans were not going to work out. I might add that at this point I had not even considered allowing time for *the book*. Off I went, undeterred.

I was back by 1:00 p.m., ate a quick lunch, and as gracefully as possible launched my canoe into the now very turbulent waters of Lake Winnipesaukee. There are a few translations for the word *Winnipesaukee*: water in a high place, smile of a great spirit, or good smooth water at an outlet. I think it really means waters where pale faces look foolish. The wind was coming on shore pretty stiffly, and the bow of the canoe kept blowing downwind. There I was with a sixteen-foot canoe, trying to row into the wind, and it was useless. I could only gain headway if I backed into the wind. I did a much better job of indicating the wind direction than I did of navigating gracefully the "waters in a high place." Better yet, the "smile of a great spirit" turned into his laughing his butt off.

Against my better judgment and with the best of intentions, I had purchased this canoe when my daughters were young. After all, camping and canoes go hand in hand. I also needed one big enough so we could all go canoeing as a happy family and carry all the supplies needed for our fifteen minutes on the water. Then, and only then, would it hang in that big empty spot in the garage until years later, when I, on the brink of senility, decided to go it alone on the wind-swept shores of a lake referred to as "good smooth waters."

After about twenty minutes of this foolishness, I could only imagine a bunch of Indian spirits standing on shore, having a good laugh. I always think of Indians when I see canoes for obvious reasons, and I always marveled at how they traveled across vast expanses of water and down rivers in canoes. Down the river is the one that gets me. How did they get back up? We use vans to bring us back to where we started. So, I finally gave up and unintentionally beached myself in almost the exact spot from which I had launched, and I exited the canoe as if it was exactly what I had planned to do. You know, in case anyone from one of the occupied campsites on the water was watching.

As I walked back up the hill, I became aware that I was not as disappointed as I felt I should be. Then it came to me; I had suspected the canoeing thing wasn't going to work out with all that wind, but I had gone for it anyway. We have all tried things against our better judgment and looked back and realize we had known what the outcome would be. Those times are the times when we get a little nudge from the other side, and we should pay attention. We all possess this knowing, but we stifle it with our egos, thinking we know better. God also has a plan for us, and we can make a choice to follow it or not. When we follow the path lit by God, we will never fail.

Written in some of the messages is the fact that God will guide with a gentle breeze. Well, I wasn't paying attention to the gentle breeze, so He kicked it up a notch. As hard as I tried, I wasn't going fishing. He had other plans. My last full day of camping was devoted to getting some of this book completed.

It is quite appropriate that the next message was where I picked up writing again. Mind you, the messages are compiled in chronological order, and I had received all of them before I started writing this book. I occasionally stopped writing the book, but I continued to receive messages. This left me with the dilemma of how this book would end. Yes, I know. I was trying to control. I should just let it happen the way it is supposed to.

The following message pertains to awareness—awareness that I didn't possess, or better still, failed to heed on my fishing endeavor. This will be one of the most important concepts to grasp: awareness. Awareness that we are spiritual beings, that every event happens for a Higher purpose, and that we are all on a similar path to enlightenment are the keys to successfully fulfilling our life purpose.

April 25, 2012

Words have been written about lessons, life's purpose, realization, recognition, revelation, and awareness. This list will go on; it must go on. For now, at this moment, the concentration on awareness will serve as the door to all other revelations in this life.

The awareness that has now begun to unfold is opening up the idea, the fact that the world in which you presently reside is not the end-all to your existence.

Through awareness you realize that you are merely a spiritual footstep away from what true life is: eternal life and the light of revelation. Through awareness you now acknowledge that there is a Divine purpose to your existence and events that occur in this lifetime.

Let this message be an exercise in that awareness. Let this message be a guide to past events and their impact on your present. Look back as far as possible to your earliest childhood memory. Do not linger in any one place; just view it and move on. This earliest memory, is it that of a parent, friend, the loss of a loved one, the loss of a pet? Whatever it is, it is an event that left an indelible mark on your soul. Was it a happy time, sad time, a time of newfound knowledge for you?

Continue on with this walk of memory. Keep moving forward toward your present place in time. Like reaching a destination, retrace the path you took on a road map and envision everything between where you started and where you have ended up.

With your newfound awareness, examine those events and look at them with a clear spiritual vision. Whatever event occurred and the emotions involved, a path was chosen that led you to where you are today. Put the pieces of the puzzle together and see how they make up who you are right now.

Past joys, past pain, past turmoil all served a Divine purpose in what you have become. Some are still going through difficult times, and others have difficulties ahead of them, but with the awareness of what is going on in this lifetime, there must be acknowledgment that all is for the best.

Now with new eyes you can look upon others. The awareness you now possess will allow you to view others as you have just viewed yourself. Is it a friend, a coworker, a loved one, or a child participating in negative activities? Do you look down on them with disdain for what they do? No, you look through the eyes of the Divine, as God does, and see them as you have seen yourself.

Events unfolding in their lives, as with yours, are to guide them on a path of awareness to where you now stand. Judgment is gone; disdain is now converted to empathy. Prayerful thoughts are sent out on their behalf as opposed to critical words spoken behind their backs.

Awareness has brought the realization that we are all on a journey, a journey to connect to our Higher Selves, our souls. As with any journey, many different paths can be taken. Many different paths must be taken for each of us to reach our destination. Fear not any event in your life, because you do not go through it alone. The presence of God and the light of heaven surround you on every step of your walk.

Choose the path with this newfound awareness that brings you to a place of higher understanding, which brings you closer to your Higher Good and the welcoming light of heaven.

Chapter 12
Through Your Actions, Not Your Words, Others Will Seek Me Out

I received the next message at work, of all places. Typically, the messages come through while I'm experiencing quiet, like when I first awaken. From this point on, the messages started to come through whenever they wanted, and now they can be triggered by any number of things, such as a song, a billboard, or a conversation, as in the case of the next message, which was channeled following a conversation with someone at work about the soon-to-be-passing of a loved one. Our thoughts are energy, and the energy of our thoughts can affect the passing of our loved ones. Not letting go of our loved ones impedes their passing and can hold back their souls' evolvement.

May 4, 2012

The passing from this world cannot be held back by the physical. The duration of your suffering is not controlled by Me; more so, it is controlled by the energies around you.

Those who love you in this physical world are the same who have loved you in the spiritual world. The lack of awareness of what true life really is, is the chain that binds you to this earth.

I seek not your endless suffering, your crippling pain, or to witness the tragedy of your passing. I seek only to comfort those around you and welcome you back from where you have come, welcome you back to the place of love and peace, a place forgotten in your human existence.

You and those around you cling to an existence that is not true life or even a real existence. Your acknowledgment of the spiritual—the true life in which you reside—is paramount to making this physical life a success.

Life here has a purpose; a reason is found in each and every event. With your newfound awareness, the perceived torments of this life gain meaning. Negatives must be experienced to know positives, evil must be experienced to know goodness, and darkness must be experienced to see the light.

Matters of this life are meaningless in what they bring to the physical but are Divinely created to bring forth the awareness, the acknowledgment, and the acceptance of the spiritual.

Change your perception of this world in which you reside. Break the thought patterns ingrained in your upbringing. Change your ideas about life and death. Acknowledge the facts that exist in your existence. Life is never ending, and the thoughts put out by you and those around you have energy. Enough energy is put out through your thoughts that events can be changed or prevented from even happening. Pray that those around you realize this, and allow yourself to break free of the grip this physical world has on you.

It is not I who prevents your passing; it is the bond created by your thoughts and the thoughts of those around you that hold you back.

Only those around you, through their acceptance of what true reality is, can allow the chains holding you back to be broken. When they release to Me what is created by Me, when they release their love of the physical, and when they acknowledge the existence of the Divine and everlasting life, they will feel the grip to this world weaken.

With a newfound awareness you will pass, not through death but through revelation to a world of true reality, true love, true peace, and everlasting life. A welcome home awaits you.

The next message contains the ever-present word: *awareness*. We must realize constantly that we are spiritual beings having a human experience. I am sure you've heard this analogy before; still we are reminded to not get too wrapped up in our physical existence and all that we seek as humans. This is not to say that we shouldn't enjoy fine things in life such as nice houses, cars, boats, etc.; instead, we must not put too much emphasis on these things. How many times have we failed to achieve something or gain something only to have it create angst in our lives for a period of time? Honestly, it has happened to me, and I'm sure it has happened to many others. We can't afford this or that, can't travel like so-and-so, I'd love a house like that—the list is endless. We go through all this, but for what purpose? When we are blessed with something special, how many times do we acknowledge who is ultimately responsible?

Truthfully, the messages I have been receiving on a fairly regular basis are more of a blessing than any earthly item I could receive. With a new sense of awareness, I doubt that anyone would not be able find something in his or her life that is a blessing that only a miracle can bring. Sit back in silence and hear what your Higher Self, your soul, is telling you. We all come from a place of Divine knowledge, an all-knowing that has been cast away in our quest for material gain.

May 9, 2012

You have been chosen to be My scribe. Not to elevate but rather to bless, you are given a gift—a gift to share. You can see what needs no eyes to see, and you can hear what needs no ears to hear. A greater awareness of your Higher Self, your soul, has been bestowed upon you. This is a gift from Me, and it can be opened by all.

The awareness you sought and still seek, the awareness others seek, and the awareness others will come to realize they too need to find is already contained in each and every one of you. Distractions in your earthly existence drown out My words. Your daily interruptions silence the communication between you and your all-knowing Higher Self.

In time you will be able to experience receiving My message in spite of what is going on around you. An example of such occurred in your workplace five days ago. Amidst the noise and confusion, I guided your hand to pen words of clarification and comfort.

Still, the awareness that all seek will come through silence. My words are clearest in silence. Communication between you and Me does not require a formal exercise as some would teach. Rather the peace and silence in your alone time is all I ask.

Sit in silence; I sit before you. On your drive to work, I sit beside you. Turn off the distractions in your life. My message is far more important than the message you receive in text, through e-mail, by phone, or on radio and TV. There are plenty of opportunities to experience this silence, even if it's only for a few minutes.

Speak to Me as you would a friend; I do not require the eloquent words of a theologian. Question Me and listen for My answer. Tell Me all about yourself, your fears, your desires, and your thoughts. Fear not My judgment, for I know your faults, your wants, your triumphs, your failures before you do. By communicating all this to Me, you give it power, you give Me power to help facilitate change.

By communicating all this, you give your Higher Self the power to pour forth its wisdom on you.

The awareness you have gained, and others will gain, can only come from the Divine. You have asked; I have answered. You have requested; I have given. Still you seek more; this too is good and as it should be. With a greater awareness come more answers. With more knowledge come more questions. With more writing come more messages.

Seek out the positive in every event. Examine your life through a magnifying glass, not to see its imperfections but more so to see the examples of goodness. Some of these opportunities were missed; others were relished. Place no judgment, as I place no judgment, on how each situation was handled. More so, seek to realize what each situation says about yourself and how or if you have evolved from it.

This self-examination will bring forth answers to questions, guidance on a new path, and a greater awareness of the purpose of life.

By now, through the series of messages so far received, one ideal has been made clear. The life that you are experiencing is not the reality of the life in which you reside, and the events in this life are not to defeat you but to guide you to who you are to become. The physical life that you are experiencing now is merely an opportunity to realize who and what you are, what is true reality as opposed to your reality, and that you as well as all others are spiritual beings on a quest of awareness, evolvement, and everlasting life.

Wow is all I can muster. All of the messages I have received are still difficult for me to wrap my mind around. I read and reread with disbelief that they came from a pen I held, and that's about all I did. I take no credit for the text; I just decided one day to write what I heard, what went through my mind, or whatever happened. I can't say I really hear a voice, but then again something, someone gets my attention. Then I write with a flow I wish I had possessed in my school years, composing some of the most far-out yet simple ideas that I have ever read. I wonder once again how our lives and the lives of those around us would change if we adopted these mind-sets. These are words of inspiration, clarification, and revelation without the fear, judgment, and restrictions so many religions place us under.

I am not shooting down anyone's religious viewpoints, and far be it for me to question the validity of any religion, but I fail to recognize the views presented within these messages in any sermon I've heard preached to the flock.

The following message sums up how simple life is. The how and why life is the way it is, is very clear. Place God first and leave your worries at His feet. We have choices, and choices made with the guidance of God serve to release us from our human tribulations.

May 26, 2012

The world in which you reside is much less complex than you make it out to be. The life in which you define yourself is much simpler than you think. Begin to see the simplicity of this existence. Release the acquisitions that do not serve your Higher Good. Relinquish the desires to attain possessions of this world and instead seek the light and truth that is found in My presence.

Through this light you will see the challenges of this life melt away. No longer will the worries, the despair, the stress of your human existence be foremost in your mind. You will recognize yourself as the spiritual being that you are. In My light you will see that each event has a specific purpose; all are opportunities to bring you closer to Me.

Your awareness to this fact will help others on their paths. Judge not those around you, for you have been where they are. They soon will be where you are, and all will be where they are supposed to be on this spiritual journey when the time is right. Each of you has different lessons and is at a different level of evolvement.

You find your words fall on deaf ears. You were once deaf. Your views cannot be seen by those who are still blind. Be the light for those in darkness; be a guide, not a judge. If I cannot force someone to find Me, surely you can't. Instead, take the route of compassion, empathy, support, understanding, awareness, and love. Through your actions, not your words, will others seek Me out.

The path has to be chosen out of free will, a gift given by Me. Too often you see free will being used selfishly as opposed to selflessly. Choices befall you many times each and every day. Freely you are given opportunities to go this way or that, to choose this or that. The angst you sometimes feel in these situations comes from the conflict between your Higher Self—your spiritual side—and your human side. One choice is not wrong; one is not right. More so, one is better for where you want to be.

The simplicity of this life is now more evident when you choose from the position of a spiritual being, which you are. The choice will always be clear. What brings you closer to Me? What serves the Highest Good for yourself and those around you?

There is only one answer to most questions you will confront in life: what is best for my Higher Self, my spirit, my soul? The choice is simple, singular, and leads you to Me.

The next message refers to our forgetting who and what we really are. It touches on the fact that we come here with a purpose, a purpose long forgotten in our human travels. Also it speaks directly to me about my questions, even the questions still coming into my mind as I write this book. Someone is watching, listening, and reading my mind when it comes to this newly discovered spirituality that I embrace. We are all the same in this forgetfulness of our spiritual selves. Some of us are better at it than others, yet we will all eventually embrace that which is true: this life is not really life. Life—true life—is on the other side.

May 26, 2012

You arrive, you exist, and you pass on. The life you experience and the purpose of it eludes many. Forgotten are the reasons you are here; forgotten is the place from which you came; and forgotten is the destination you seek through this life. Many around you fail to accept, understand, and take hold of the messages passed on to you. Even you yourself question at times the validity of what you receive. You are born into this world with a knowing, a remembrance of your spiritual existence. With curiosity, you seek to experience all this new world has to offer.

To your detriment, you lose touch with your true reality. Wrapped up in the trappings of this human existence, you become enveloped in being human, and your spiritual connection, although unbroken, is forgotten. Many still feel a connection to the Divine but remain unsure, unconvinced, or unworthy. Do not seek out your answers through theologies that attempt to condemn, place guilt, or control. Seek the path of healing, compassion, and love.

Each and every one of you possesses the power to evolve, to evolve from the daily grind of your existence to a place of peace and harmony. You all possess an indestructible spiritual energy that can transform even the most misguided among you.

This spiritual connection, long forgotten on your walk through this life, contains a reservoir of healing power. Your actions, your words, and most of all your thoughts, have an energy behind them that can be a catalyst for change. Positive thoughts, words, and actions must be foremost in your existence here.

Negative events in this lifetime are the roadblocks that redirect your path. Divine instinct, intuition that you all possess, gravitates toward the positive. When negative events, people, or conditions present themselves, make note of the warning sign. Examine yourself; ask God, *Where am I going wrong? Why must I endure?* The roadblocks were put there to redirect, to redirect you toward God and your Source. Like the beautiful, happy young baby that develops into the cynical, angry adult, a wrong turn was made; a warning sign was ignored.

Through acceptance and the knowing that a Higher Power exists, redemption is in the offering. Blessed are those who accept, acknowledge, and welcome Divine changes in their lives.

The world as you know it—the physical, the scientific—is merely a box you have placed yourself in. By not remembering who and what you truly are, you have created a prison in which to reside. No matter how wonderful a life you have been blessed with, it pales in comparison to the life you had, are having, and will continue to have in the light of God.

The existence of God, as viewed by many, remains unproven. In the same token, God's existence cannot be disproven either. Where then do the inspiration, the healing, the drive, the messages, and the unexplained originate? Are they merely quirks of nature or imagination, or is it just happenstance that each and every one of you possesses different goals, desires, and life experiences? Is it that you yourself at some arbitrary place in your life just started to receive thoughts and messages that in many ways didn't reflect your life up until that point?

Look outside the box you live in. Step out of the box society has created, and step into the light of God. For there the path is clear, roadblocks are removed, and the walk of faith becomes an everyday experience.

We must make a choice to remove ourselves from the boxes we have created in our lives. The comfort zones to which we so readily retreat must be expanded to include new experiences, new people, and in some cases new viewpoints. I have had to continue to write what I have received with an open mind, something that wasn't always apparent in me until I started getting these messages. I still at times retreat to some of my old ways; it is not that they were that bad, but they pale in comparison to how I view life now.

The final message in this chapter is a message that drives home the fact that we are all loved by God, regardless of what we have become. Some people need to hear this. The God that is vengeful, judgmental and at the ready with lightning bolts to destroy the world does not exist. We ultimately have the control over our lives through the choices we make, but once again we must place God first in our decision making to really serve our life purpose.

May 28, 2012

Does it seem rational that I, the God in which you believe, would create beings such as yourself—imperfect in many ways—place you in an imperfect world, and then expect perfection? Would I then seek to punish the failures that are inevitable? What God, what father, would set a child up for failure?

It is not perfection that I seek from you; more so, it is awareness and revelation I seek for you through the experiences that this life brings forth. During each and every event, whether perceived positively or negatively by you, I stand at the ready for support and to receive thanks from you.

Each and every event in your life, large or small, provides you with an opportunity to make a decision. Each event, Divinely created, grants you an opportunity to see Me and include Me in your life. The free will of which I have spoken before is the gift granted by Me, your Creator, for you to achieve the highest level of spiritual evolvement. It can also lead you astray.

Not surprising to Me, the path you choose to take is yours alone. I do not judge; I only remain steadfast for support and guidance when asked. I already know the path you're going to choose. I already know the trials you will suffer through. I already know the time and place when you will acknowledge My existence and seek Me out.

For Me to punish you would be pointless. The right and wrong that your world so readily judges is only important in your eyes, not Mine. The importance in choices made by you through free will is the experience that was gained. What exactly does your choice say about you and what you have become through your exercise in free will?

To evolve to a place of peace, joy, and love that so many and ultimately all in your world seek, a free choice to acknowledge My existence must be made. I must be sought out freely. Not through fear, intimidation, guilt, or control can My light be revealed. Insomuch as you are controlled, you will control. Through control, you will resist, and through resistance, you will rebel.

There are those among you who find themselves in just such a situation. Those of you who have found Me are to be the guides for those who are lost. Your actions will speak louder than your words, and opportunity will present itself for you to openly acknowledge My works in your life. Wait patiently for those who seek Me to ask. Your actions will open minds, and your words will open eyes.

Continue forth with Me first and foremost in your mind. In each decision, in each word spoken, and in each event, find My presence. Do not labor in any one event and question why; instead be thankful for the opportunity to experience Me in a very special way.

For those of you who are suffering, I cannot crash through the door to save you. Instead I will be the light breeze that gets your attention for you to make a choice to freely seek Me out, to see Me in a new light. You alone are responsible for your salvation.

Keeping Me first and foremost in your thoughts and choices will in turn grant you the awareness of your Divine interconnectedness—our interconnectedness. By welcoming Me freely into your life, your heart will grant you the healing and wholeness you seek. What better gift can you give yourself and those around you than to experience the completeness, the joy, and the peace that this life can provide through My grace?

This passage reinforces that through our free will, we must make choices to go one way or the other in regard to our own spiritual awakening. We in some ways are less than perfect as humans. However, we must remember that our humanness is not true life. Our true life exists within our souls, our spiritual sides, which are part and parcel of God and each other. This point is the important part of the puzzle that we seem to forget.

Chapter 13
Give to Me the Burdens I Seek to Carry for You

The next passage is very clear in its effort to point out that my viewpoints have changed and that those who have read these messages have changed their viewpoints as well. Some of what was channeled speaks of a God who is nonjudgmental—quite a twist from what we have all been brought up believing. It's hard to believe that anything goes, and really it doesn't. Instead, we are the makers of our own spiritual futures. The more awareness we have right now, the more evolved we become in each lifetime and the better spiritually for us. When we keep God first and foremost in our decision making, it is all quite easy—in theory, of course. With all our human frailties, our personal material desires, and the influence of our egos, the choices aren't always easy to make. This does not mean that any choice that benefits only our human existence is bad or that we should live a life of martyrdom. We have to be aware of the choices that bring us closer to God and realize the blessings He bestows upon us daily. I never asked to receive such insight, but I must make myself aware that something pretty big is going on here, and with this I have a responsibility to share these messages. It took a while for me to get on the bandwagon, and now I see no option other than to go along for the ride. My guides are speaking, and I have been blessed with the ability to hear them. What more can anyone ask?

June 16, 2012

By now, through the messages you have received, the world has become a much different place than the world you arrived in. Your views and the views of those who have read these messages are now much different. The purpose of life, the events surrounding your existence, and the life cycle of those around you have a much deeper meaning. An awareness has befallen you and those around you, which helps to explain the unexplainable and console the inconsolable.

What are you? How would you answer that? A doctor, a lawyer, a teacher, a secretary, an accountant, etc., were—and in some cases are—the first things that came to mind. Why not answer more accurately? I am spirit, I am a Divine being, and I am a child of God.

Yes, the looks you would receive from some are familiar to us, your guides. Better responses for now may be the following: I am a father, I am a mother, I am a friend, I am a brother, I am a sister, I am a husband, or I am a wife. Seek not to describe yourself as the something that provides you your income or something that you do. Instead, the profession you have chosen is something that you've chosen to do, not become. Was this choice rooted in personal growth or personal gain? Did you choose your career path to better your ability to serve others or to gain an experience that would aid in your greater awareness?

Now look at yourself carefully. Look deep inside and ask yourself, *Is this what I really want? Is this what I really need?* In youth, your motivations are much different than they are after you've aged, gained wisdom, and experienced the life you've chosen.

Is your worth to others only in what you can provide materially? Do you have the best of everything and still can't find the peace and happiness you sought? Be grateful for this awareness. You are getting in touch with your Higher Self, your soul, and its true purpose of being here. Have you ever noticed that in a lot of cases, those with the least have a spiritual conviction that can't be broken? They are aware of God and the blessings He bestows on us daily. They pray to Him and thank Him each and every day. The awareness that God is in control has not eluded them; they are blessed.

All can find this awareness. Are you blessed with material wealth? Be grateful to God and seek the purpose behind His gifts. This can be said about any life situation, whether perceived positively or negatively. Each and every event is orchestrated for you to gain the awareness of who and what you really are and to acknowledge who is in control. Release yourself from the chains you have created to bind you to this existence. Release the ego and humble yourself to God and those around you.

One person is not greater or lesser, better or worse, worthy or unworthy based on the path he or she has chosen. More so, the path you have chosen will speak volumes about what you have become. You have arrived here as a child of God, and your experiences in this life were put in place to assess your awareness of who and what you truly are. How have you done so far?

If you were to return to your place of origin with God, would you walk through heaven's gates with your head held high or hung down in shame? God already knows the answer. He knows each and every misstep you have taken and will take. He has already forgiven. You are His child, a child of God. What better way to describe who you are?

Now is your opportunity to show your thanks in words and actions. The path can always be altered but never lengthened. The end may be off in the distance or right around the corner. The light of heaven can best be seen with your head held high.

We have just been given a little insight regarding what it might take to find happiness in this life. When you view yourself accurately, you will come to realize who and what each and every one of us is. We are spiritual beings and part of God. Now you must ask how your present life fits into this new person you see yourself as. There are many who are blessed with abundance, yet they cannot find true happiness. Why is this? Are they living their lives in accordance to their souls' purpose? Are they, are we, using the gifts given to them by our Creator for the betterment of others? I am not going to attempt to answer for anyone, but we must realize that our skills, wealth, and intelligence are all gifts from God to be used in a way that is helpful to others. I personally have found more peace and happiness with a changed mind-set than with anything else I have done up to this point.

Once again, a message—the next message—hit home on events that were occurring in my life. This particular time I was quite frustrated with a lot of things. We have all experienced times when we look back at choices we have made and regret them. Be it our careers, personal decisions, or financial choices, our egos can at times make us feel quite inadequate. This was one of those times. I debated a major purchase, whined about not having the financial resources I thought I should have, looked at my business, and just could not wait to get out. Instead of looking at all I had, I created an imaginary world of lack.

God hears and knows all that is occurring in our lives. His message came to me quite clearly on June 21, 2012. Many of these messages, and this one in particular, spoke to me directly and gently put me in my place. Basically, we need to relinquish control to God, and everything else falls into place. When we give up trying to control, we also remove worry from our lives. After all, when has worry accomplished anything positive? I once read somewhere that when we worry, we prevent God from doing His job. Most of all, we must master the ability to recognize the difference between needs and wants.

June 21, 2012

The quest upon which you have embarked, in your eyes, may seem to be fruitless. The paths you take are not taken alone. I accompany you on each and every path you choose. As a companion or as a guide, I stand beside you every step of the way.

Your knowledge of what you want clouds the knowledge that awareness brings. The wants that you pursue distract you from the needs that you require. In the quest for wants, I am your companion. In the quest for needs, I am your guide. As your companion in your quest for wants, I comfort you in your disappointments, failures, and shortcomings. As your guide, I lead. I lead you to awareness, recognition, and the realization of what you need and what you are.

Through the acknowledgment of need and acceptance of My guidance, you will attain all that is blessed on earth and in heaven. Only through the guidance I offer and the satisfactions of needs that I can provide will the wants in your life be realized.

Relinquish the control you think you possess to Me. Experience the liberation of letting go and letting Me carry My end of the log. Humble yourself and stand before Me in acceptance of what is.

Through Me you achieve greatness. Through Me you achieve peace. Through Me you find happiness. I am your light; allow Me to shine. The path to completeness is found through My guidance.

Like insects drawn to a light, come out of the darkness of control and into the light of awareness, acknowledgment, and acceptance. I am the Source. I am the light. I am the all. Give to Me the burdens I seek to carry for you. Allow Me to be your guide every second of every day, and experience the release provided when your worries are placed at My feet.

You must purposely relinquish the control you think you have over your life to Me. For it is I who has always and forever will be in control. Knowing this, a conscious choice must be made by you, not to give up but to give in to the life I can provide you.

Accept where I've placed you, accept the challenges before you, and accept My guidance with a knowing that the best for you comes through your allowing My presence in your life.

CHAPTER 14
I AM SPIRIT; I AM ONE WITH GOD

The next message I received had me worried. *Is this the last one? I've just gotten to the point that I am not questioning what I write. Could it be that this is my imagination? Or worse, am I crazy?*

There was no need for me to worry. I was being told that it was time to get off the fence and to decide once and for all what I believed. The messages continued, but if I had not made the choice, their meaning would have eluded me. I basically had to practice what had been preached and include in my daily life all the ideals contained in my writings. I guess at this point you, the reader, have either opened your mind to these messages and are looking at things a little differently, or you closed the book pages ago. Either way, it's all good. If need be, you'll get another chance in your next life.

July 8, 2012

You and those of you who have read the messages brought forth have reached a threshold, a precipice. Now is the time that you must make a choice. You must leap, and you must sign on the dotted line. You must accept these ideals—these truths—into your life and move forward. How negatively would your life be affected by following the path all the preceding messages have brought you on? How negatively would your life be affected if you did not?

A very different view of life and your world has been presented. Heaven has been spoken about; a heaven that many already believed existed but now find the requirements to enter are much different. Everlasting life, something many already believed in, is a much different concept now. God, a being most profess to believe in, is now a being that we know.

No longer are the ways of God mysterious, and no longer is heaven a place of welcome for only those who have achieved perfection or suffered in the name of God. No longer are those around us judged harshly or judged at all, because the recipients of these messages see others as they see themselves: souls on a journey of evolvement, struggling to gain awareness and seeking to live in the light. No longer is the ladder of life to be climbed by stepping on others.

Constantly in your daily life there are choices. Many times you will hear some say, "I had no choice" or "It was the only choice." There is never only one choice, but there is only one choice that is best for your evolvement. The time has come for you to make that *best* choice. Enough has been written to explain, clarify, and enlighten you about the purpose of life.

No, this is not the end of the messages you will receive; more so, this is the point at which an acknowledgment must be made by yourself and those around you. Accept that this is the way it must be; this is the way it is. Further messages will be lost if the basic concept of everlasting life, being one with God, and unconditional love are not accepted.

No longer are the basic facts of who and what you are and how and why it all happens necessary. No longer is the excuse "I'm only human" acceptable. Now the excuse will be "I was only acting human." These will be your new code words for someone on your same path: "Sorry. I was acting human."

Those are the words spoken by someone who is, although struggling with this existence, living in Spirit, living in awareness, living in recognition, and living in the realization that the world he or she was brought up in is not the real world.

There is always a "the time has come" moment, and this is it. Make the choice, turn belief into knowing, and embrace the you that you have become.

At this point a thought about fear came into my mind. It will really be quite obvious once I explain. Most everything in our lives here on earth is controlled on some level by fear. We don't speed because we're afraid to get a ticket, we pay our utilities on time or risk being shut off, and we pay our mortgages or lose our houses.

The economy is bad; I can be laid off. The list is endless. Then we walk into church and we are told of God's judgment: we must go to confession, fast on Fridays, or what have you. I don't think it's as bad as it was in my parent's day when the nuns in Catholic school could have almost arranged the meeting with your maker, but the control by fear and guilt is still there.

Through the messages so far and future ones, we now see—or at least I have the belief—that the only thing not controlled by fear or guilt is our relationship with God. This is the opposite of what we have been brought up to believe. God does not seek a relationship with us out of guilt or fear but out of love. I would not want my children to respect me or seek me out because of guilt or fear but rather because they love me and value my presence. So far I think that's working out pretty well. From what I can tell from these writings, our relationship with God is pretty much the same.

No longer do I believe that God will pass judgment on me or anyone else and banish us to an eternity of suffering. What parent could do that to a child? I could see instances in which I might be displeased or even disgusted with my children's choices, but I could never stop loving my children. God is pretty much the same from what I can tell.

Standing by our side constantly, many times disappointed but always loving and forgiving, God's greatest gift to us is His patience. For those times when He can't take it one second longer, He sends His guardian angels to protect us from our own stupidity. Truthfully, I think God has a sense of humor and that some souls are here purely for His entertainment. Other than the last few sentences, I think this reflection was Divinely placed.

More than a month elapsed before I was channeled another message. It happened to be on a Sunday, as many of them are. I don't know if that holds any significance or just that it is my one day off and I try to force myself to sleep an hour or so later? Even though I receive these messages at random times, I see now that they come through much clearer when I'm in that relaxed state. The day-to-day distractions sometimes hinder the flow of messages, but I realize that this is something I have to work on. We all must teach ourselves to stay in a state of awareness to hear, see, and recognize the Divinely placed events in our lives. Like a whisper in my ear, I heard the first two sentences of the following message.

August 12, 2012

You have missed receiving messages. You have thought, *Are they over? Has whoever it's been that has been giving me these thoughts, these messages … are they gone?* No, you have left. You have left to reside in the physical world that many of you still have difficulty separating from.

The day-to-day events of work, kids home from school, and acquisition of the material have clouded your vision and obstructed your path. You are not the only one; many waiver between physical awareness and spiritual awareness. Many more remain stuck in the physical.

Your car runs out of gas, and you open the door and begin to walk to your destination. It may be a long walk or a short one. It may be difficult because you're tired, it's snowing, or it's a hot summer day. Nevertheless, the transition from driving to walking is seamless and has no effect on the vehicle. The vehicle has no importance if it cannot function to serve you.

The same is true for you in regards to your passing from this world. You leave your body when it can no longer serve you or when you have reached the destination you seek. There is a seamless transition from physical life to life in spirit because, truly, your spiritual existence has never and could never cease to exist.

Death—or better put, passing—has never been an end; it has always been and will always be a continuation. This is the point where the attachment to the physical aspect of your world can cause the most heartache. Because of the lack of spiritual awareness, you hold on to the memories of the physical presence of that loved one. Possessions of the person who has passed become reminders, mementos, and sometimes even small monuments to who they were. Your gravitation toward the physical once again becomes a stumbling block on your path and your loved one's path to awareness.

You are all energetic beings, spirits with a purpose known only to you and God. This energy, your soul, is what propels you on your path and is everlasting. The souls of your loved ones, unseen in your physical world, are only an arm's length away. So close yet so distant, there are many who have been able to tap into the ability to reach out and feel, hear and communicate with those who have passed. This does not occur on the physical level but on the energetic level. All of you are energy, all of you are one, and all of you are part of God.

Life on earth, when viewed from the physical, makes you appear to be separate from others. You are your own body, your own mind, free to do as you please, but that is not truly the case. You are an energetic being, a soul. Your energy can be felt, and your thoughts put out energy. You pick up on others' energy and can be positively or negatively affected by it. Everyone has experienced the positive or negative feelings produced when someone enters a room, when you meet someone for the first time, or when a disagreement occurs.

Become more aware of those times, concentrate more on the energetic level, and bring yourself to a higher awareness and away from the physical. A handshake, a loving embrace, and physical intimacy is not pleasurable for what it brings to the physical; more so, it serves to give you an opportunity to feel the energetic exchange between two people—a connection that brings forth the awareness of our energetic connection to each other and God. We are one.

Begin to leave the trappings of the material world behind. That is not to say that you should not enjoy the gifts given to you by God, but instead seek to find time in solitude to connect to your Higher Self and to God. More positive energy is found standing next to an animal, on a beach deserted of people, or alone in a forest than can be found in a mall full of people. The energetic life force from beings who live in the now will do more to calm you than anything created by man. The vastness of the oceans and the unseen forces that control it will give you the strength you need to persevere. The solitude of the forest and the life force it contains is impossible not to feel. From the mightiest tree to the most fragile of its insects, the energy combined in such a place will ground you and grant you a new perspective on life.

Everyone and every place contain energy. You are a limitless power supply—an everlasting life in need of a new perspective. Send it out the best way you know how, through yourself, through these messages, through God.

You have strayed from your path yet still know your way. You have helped others with your words while ignoring yourself. You are aware that you have forgotten. So all in all, that's not bad for the imperfect being the illusion in your mind portrays you as, but it is bad.

Each and every one of you contains—and is—the perfection that only God can create. The separation from your spiritual side, thus your separation from God, is what causes your imperfections. Repeat daily the following:

I am spirit. I am one with God. We are all one with each other.

This was the most difficult message to write since you've been receiving. The messages will continue and become more difficult. Leave your vehicle, walk through the snow or the heat or whatever impedes your progress, but do not stop. Reach your destination for yourself and then for others. The physical lies behind; life lies ahead.

I'm sure you're seeing a trend here; the first few sentences sum it up. It's my fault, and misery loves company, so it's your fault too. I am residing in the physical world. What else are we supposed to do?

We must stay aware, aware that we are not just flesh and bone but spiritual beings. Our life is not just this life; we have eternal life in a place not of this world. It was written in one of the earlier messages that heaven is part of earth, but earth can never be a part of heaven. I see now that the part of heaven that is earth is us. I always wondered what that meant. Well, we are spiritual beings, we have come from heaven, and we each carry the light of God in us. Heaven is not just a place to which we go; it is also a place from which we come.

Now, what of this world can we bring back? Nothing. I once heard someone joke that this is why hearses don't have luggage racks. Seriously though, we all know that any earthly possessions stay behind, and the only thing we can take back are our lessons learned.

The next message is one of forgiveness. Forgiveness is something that seems to be the major lesson we must master to truly evolve to a place of peace and happiness in this world and the next.

August 14, 2012

Forgiveness flows with the grace and ease of a skater on a frozen pond. You, and many like you, have discovered the awareness that life is supposed to bring you—the awareness that you are spirit, all are spirit. This life is not true life, and we are all actors in this play called life.

The dance that is life is perfectly choreographed so that forgiveness opportunities present themselves to you on a regular basis. With the awareness of who and what you are, it is difficult to understand the hesitation to forgive others.

This life in which you presently reside is nothing more than a play. Each of you is an actor and plays a specific role. Each of you comes here with a soul purpose to play a specific part. You are a wife, a husband, a child with disabilities, an addict, a teacher, whatever and every person you meet, every situation you encounter is orchestrated to open up a forgiveness opportunity.

The time has come for you and others to view your existence in this way. You and each and every person you meet is a spirit, a soul residing here to evolve, to progress to a higher level of awareness. Past messages have spoken of this; yet in your daily lives, it is forgotten. The events of this life are not put in place to destroy, separate, or impede; more so, the events you experience are used to assess how far you have come.

All of you, and that means each and every person on this planet, is part and parcel of God and contains all the perfection that comes with being created by God. What you have forgotten and what you have allowed yourself to become is the impediment that obstructs your path. God does not create the negativity in your life; you do. God does not produce the anger, resentment, judgment, or even the happiness and joy in life; you do. Through your greater awareness of who and what you are and your connection to God and the Divine, the joy that this life provides can be recognized. A conscious choice must be made by each as to how he or she is going to view this existence.

The joys of this life seem to elude many. The sick, the poor, the disabled, the shunned, and the challenged people of this world show you the pain and suffering that is life. But when viewed from the perspective of a greater awareness of what life truly is—that we are spirit, one with God in heaven— our true life is perfect. What you experience here is not the reality of your existence. Each of you has come here with a purpose and an experience you need to contend with to evolve to a higher level. Each of you crosses paths with others at specific points in your life to give you opportunities to experience joys and as an opportunity to forgive.

When viewing yourself as a spiritual being in this existence right now and realizing that all that bothers, offends, or causes suffering is not the true reality of life, it is extremely easy to offer forgiveness to others and see the greater picture in the negative experiences in life.

Forgiveness to yourself and others should flow like water, flow with the grace and ease of a skater on ice. Through making a conscious choice to view life as a play, the reality of which is created in our own minds, forgiveness is a simple yet powerful gift to give. The joy that is found in choosing to live in the light of God brings you happiness. The joy that is found in choosing to forgive releases you from your burdens. Look at the bigger picture. Grant the gift that's so freely given to you each and every day by God to others you meet. Your rise to a greater awareness, to realization, and to heaven starts with releasing your burdens.

We are told that forgiveness should not necessarily be easy but that more so it should flow freely. Holding on to grudges, resentment, and anger does not aid one bit in our spiritual evolvement. I now look at anger and such as walking around with a backpack on all day. You carry this load around with you. It constantly gets heavier and heavier, and you are the only one who knows what is contained within it. Many times the person who has offended us, knowingly or unknowingly, has no idea of what we're carrying around. So off we go on our walk through life, weighed down by the pain contained within, only to become more stressed, angrier, and more resentful.

We can and must give ourselves a gift: forgiveness. By forgiving you are putting down the burden of pain and anger for yourself and for others. No longer will you walk through life with that proverbial chip on your shoulder for all to see. Forgive yourself, first and foremost, for feeling the way you do and realize that you are just "acting" human. The awareness that we are works in progress and that our true purpose here is not what we gain on the material level is the key to removing our ego from the picture and offering our forgiveness to all around us. After all, if all our sins can and are forgiven by God, who are we to give so much power to others' wrongs against us? Forgiveness is a gift you give to yourself.

The next message came at a time when I was questioning why some people face such difficulties in life. My wife had an appointment to see a Reiki client, which was scheduled immediately following her client's appointment with her doctor about a serious illness. My wife never comes home and tells me specifics of anyone's situation, but this day she wanted to tell me of the joy she had witnessed.

This particular person had received serious news from her doctor and had mentioned this to my wife before the visit. As my wife approached her client's home, she could hear music playing, and as she was ushered into the house, she saw her client dancing with her husband. It was her birthday, and they were celebrating with some friends and their two-year-old daughter. My wife stepped into a home filled with energy so positive that she could feel it. After receiving such disappointing news, this couple was living in the moment and dancing to their wedding song with their daughter. My wife questioned why she herself could not feel such joy at times, since our life was not consumed by doctor visits and prognoses.

My wife called me to tell me of the experience she had been a part of, and I couldn't control the wave of emotion that came over me on my drive home. I felt happy for them and sad for them and wondered why this all has to be so difficult. Also, why did I get so darn emotional over things that really had no bearing on my life?

On my drive home, I passed the cemetery where my grandparents are buried, and where else would you ask questions about such things? If anyone was hiding behind a gravestone, they would have thought I was nuts. I got out of my truck and walked around the cemetery, asking—challenging—any soul who had passed to stand before me and explain to me first why I had such strong emotions over this situation and secondly why this family had to go through such heartache. Why was I so upset about someone I didn't know and the thought that this person might not survive? After all, those who have passed are privy to the Divine information we all seek, right?

Instead there was silence. Of course, the cemetery is not where the deceased reside, so what was I thinking? Well, after about a half hour of this nonsense, I drove home without my answer. It came the next morning.

August 16, 2012

You have asked a question and boldly sought an answer. You expected—you challenged—those who have passed to stand before you and give you all the answers you need. This did not happen in a physical sense, but you are now receiving the answer you sought.

This question, and all questions, can be answered through the messages you have so far received. This is not to imply that all Divine knowledge has been granted to you, but enough to facilitate your awareness has been bestowed on you so far.

Beliefs in your present existence come through two very different mind-sets. There is the belief that something is real or true because you want it to be or the belief that something is true because you know it to be true. Here is the spot at which you and many others reside.

By now, with the events of the last five years that you have experienced, you have moved much closer to the knowing than ever before. Once again, a choice presents itself, and you must turn one way or the other. "How?" You haven't spoken it, but I hear it in your mind.

All knowledge is contained within your Higher Self—your soul. Your soul knows the direction to turn, the path to take. Like memories of childhood events, your remembrance of your spiritual life has been washed away to the furthest reaches of your mind. Never gone but far from reach, the waters that retain the knowledge of your spiritual existence lie deep within. Dig deep, release the waters of knowledge you all possess, and the questions that remain will be washed away. Left behind will not be new knowledge but a remembrance, a recollection of a place of peace, healing, forgiveness, and love.

Tears will be shed with the passing of a loved one, but they will be tears of joy, not of sorrow. The spiritual connection you have with a loved one that has passed is closer and stronger than the physical connection you have to one that has moved across town.

You are on the right path. Questions are stumbling blocks. When you were a child, you believed what you were told by elders, and that is part of the problem. Some of what has been spoken became fact in your eyes, and you now know that is not always true. Still you must retain your childlike presence when you stand before God. Hear what He has to say and know that it is the truth. Experience what He has in store for you and know it is for the best. Through great faith in your path and in God, no questions will remain, and the eternal peace, joy, happiness, and love that you deserve will be yours.

Someone obviously heard me. Now we have to read between the lines a bit to get the answer. I have found that many of the messages we receive and the signs that are all around us are not as obvious as we would like. This is not how the spiritual realm works. I don't really hear someone speaking to me the way I would if I was sitting across a table from someone. Instead, it is a thought or words in my head that get my attention.

Basically it boils down again to the fact that what we are experiencing right at this moment is not really life. Just as you sit in front of a television and watch a movie, what you see is not reality. Still, we can get so wrapped up in a movie that our emotions can get the better of us. We are all actors in this play called life, and this is an educational program we are starring in. All of us are here to teach and to learn, so don't put too much drama into the scene you are in because, in essence, it's not true reality.

This is not to say we should walk through life emotionless about everything around us. Instead, we should experience events but not let them interfere with our path. I am specifically referring to the negative emotions of anger, jealousy, and sorrow. Anger and jealousy fall under the forgiveness mind-set. Sorrow falls under the belief—the knowing—that life never really ends. The hole created by the grief felt when someone is seriously ill or has passed can only be filled with the realization that life is eternal. We never die, and the ones who have crossed are closer to us than we realize.

My wife also has her hurdles to cross, and she still suffers from some of the physical effects of going through major surgeries twenty-some odd years ago. When taking a walk one afternoon, she questioned, "What is it that I need to do to not experience the physical aches and pains anymore?" At times she doesn't feel the joy that her Reiki client had felt dancing away at home after hearing such disappointing news from the doctor. The joy and the ability to live for the moment elude many of us. Aches and pains, worries about the future, and everyday stress cause us to lose sight of what is really occurring in what we call life. She questioned aloud, "Does it ever end, and how long must I endure …?"

After receiving an answer to my last question specifically, we wondered if some message would come through on this one. We were not disappointed.

August 19, 2012

The discomforts you experience on a human level in the past, now, and in the future, both emotional and physical, are nothing more than stepping stones on your path of ascension. Mapped out by you, they are mile markers on a journey of your choosing. Ever present is the light of God, although many times far off, reachable just the same.

The path that you and all are on is the path to true spiritual awareness. Each and every one of you will attain it. Most will come to this realization at their passing, and there are some who will come to know it in this lifetime. Some have already reached this point—the point where the realization that the body and the events that it partakes in are not truly life.

Right now to experience, touch, feel, and be part of the spiritual realm seems to be out of reach, a place that can only be experienced through your passing. Some will challenge that idea; some have conquered it. Referred to as masters, there are those who reside in this world who are capable of consciously removing themselves from the negative experiences of their lives, both physical and emotional, and residing in a place of total peace.

The one for whom this message was prompted has questioned specifically the events in this lifetime. The one for whom this message was prompted already has differing views of the events that make up this lifetime. More and more peace is sought in this soul's life experience.

From the beginning, this soul has been challenged and placed itself, once again, to be challenged in this lifetime. Events have conditioned this soul to choose a certain path, a path now realized as not the best for its evolvement. In the past, and even in the farthest past, this soul has questioned why, has felt different, misunderstood, and not connected to those around it. This continuation of confusion is what is coming to an end. The stifling of positive emotions will be released with the breath of God, and the opportunity to open the gift of peace is at hand. To phrase it a little more clearly, this soul has been offered the opportunity of dual citizenship by becoming a resident of the physical world and the spiritual world at the same time.

Healing came to and through this soul from the Divine. The path this soul has chosen to walk proves difficult through its simplicity, is unclear because it is so obvious, and is unattainable because it has been reached. Once again, perspective must be changed, burdens must be released, and an awakening will occur. The discomforts of the present are, and will be shown to be, inconsequential. The ability to fully realize will be granted, but for now view all events as assessments. Are you ready for what is being offered, and are you prepared to carry the light to others?

What you have experienced and what you are about to experience does not exist in your present sense of time. You will come to realize what has taken forever to achieve happened very quickly, and what has occurred quickly has been in the works for lifetimes. Whether you are worthy or unworthy or deserve or do not deserve are no longer questions that need answers. Walls have come down; now climb upon the rubble of your past pain, hurts, and disillusionment and gaze upon the glory of two worlds merging. Walk through the gate that swings both ways, for the key has been created for you. The ability to leave this world while still being a part of it has been gifted to you. Open it and enjoy.

Although this message is an answer to one particular soul's question, you who received it are on a similar path of awareness. Both of you are separate but walk together, and both of you lead while you lag behind. The amazement you both exhibit in regard to events in your lives is just an example of your inability to receive the gifts given to you by God with a realization that you are deserving and qualified to possess and share such gifts. Past human conditioning and mind-sets have brought about this sense of unworthiness, but you and all are worthy of God's blessings. You both have sought these blessings, asked for the blessings, and earned these blessings. Leave the amazement to nonbelievers and enjoy now where you reside. Look forward to the future and the blessings in store, for truer words have never been spoken: "You ain't seen nothing yet!"

Not knowing specifics about my wife's past, it is still easy to see that this response from Spirit was directed toward her. Both of us received a message in the last paragraph. We both are demonstrating different abilities when it comes to interaction with the Divine, and we should not question how or why we have been chosen. Be it the receiver of messages or the gift of being attuned to be a Reiki practitioner, we—and all of us—are deserving of the gifts given to us by God. So drop the old mind-sets and accept the reality that gifts have been and will continue to be given to those who follow their souls' chosen path. Miracles do happen through channeling, and healing does occur through energy work.

CHAPTER 15
RESIDE IN THE LIGHT THAT IS GOD

The following message, which I received a number of days later, speaks to what is necessary to have God in our lives. It is not really difficult, and if you leave the slightest opening in your life, God will find His way to you.

September 2, 2012

The breeze through which God travels will fit through the tiniest of spaces. It is you who must provide the opening.

Situations that impede, stifle, or prevent your forward movement are also the same situations that propel you forward when the grace of God breathes in your direction. You alone must be the one to open the window, even if slightly, and let the cooling breeze of an autumn night into your life. You must commit to the change you seek. Through your thoughts, words, and actions the pain that is discipline is only temporary. God will do what you yourself cannot do, but you must make the first move: open the window and allow God to enter.

The pain of compromise is permanent. What-ifs, should-haves, and could-haves will be the painful reminders of missed opportunities. Your dreams, your goals, your desires, when viewed in God's light, are His gifts to us; not bestowed on us freely, these gifts are ours for the asking. Through patience, perseverance, and faith we must demonstrate our commitment to God and His grace, and He will provide.

Remove the negative influences in your life, become deaf to those who do not elevate your spirit, and become blind to the situations that hold your evolvement back.

Reside in the light that is God—all-knowing and the provider of all. Seek out like-minded people to brighten further the light that you need in your life. Leave behind the people, places, and situations that hold you back. Judge not the aforementioned; only judge how you are affected by residing under the influences of such situations.

By constantly moving forward, you follow those who have lead the way and keep open the path for others to follow, if they so choose. Do not be stymied by misdirected sympathies or guilt placed on you by others. The compassion you possess is a gift from God to help you bring others to Him, not to hold you back.

Choosing a path illuminated by the best and the brightest of God's light is always the right path. Once again you must choose wisely. Humble yourself and ask for strength, perseverance, wisdom, guidance, and realization. Open the window ever so slightly and allow God to creep into your life. Demonstrate your commitment to all that is good, and you shall receive. Soon you will come to the realization that the perceived sacrifices and missed opportunities were really impediments on your ever-evolving walk in God's light. All of life's questions will have answers when this newfound realization becomes first and foremost in your life.

An awareness has been gifted to you and to those who read these messages—a gift from God for your faith, a gift for listening, and a gift for writing. What was once a chore has become a necessary and welcomed part of your existence. What was once thought of as a sacrifice is now viewed as a blessing. What is viewed as difficult or impossible in human terms is always for the best and possible when viewed through the eyes of God.

The professed belief that God knows best is one thing, but to see the blessing in each and every event is something much different. Your eyes and the eyes of others are beginning to open. Prepare to be blind to all that you thought was real, and welcome into your life all that *is* real. What seems insurmountable is possible when you choose to have faith in yourself and faith in God. The impossible is what makes miracles possible.

Open the window. Open it wide. Throw open the door and walk into a world of untold possibilities with God at your side.

This message once again reminds us that we must create an opening for God to enter into our lives. Even the smallest effort will grant God a foothold, and all the events in our lives will be blessed by Him. It is through our free will that the choice must be made. God will not storm in and take over our lives. Our paths, when walked in communion with God, will have His blessing. Awareness to this simple fact is in itself a gift from God, and through this awareness we will also come to realize that even the most difficult times in our lives hold hidden blessings.

This last message seems to sum up exactly what needed to be said by Spirit, God, and whoever guided my hand to pen these messages. Some of the messages were simple examples of the way life can be described, while others had a much deeper meaning for me and those with whom I have shared them.

Never before have I been so compelled to complete a task, and never before have had I held such a fear about how something I've done will be viewed. So with trepidation I went forward and shared these messages, some of which were directed solely at me. I questioned myself many times as to whether or not I should continue with this and if I did, how I would know when I should end it. I left it in God's hands to guide me to completion, and the last message in this book seems perfect, a simple yet powerful message: leave a place for God in your life.

Throughout the last few years of receiving messages like this, I wondered if I was fantasizing or even hallucinating at times; however, events unfolded around me that confirmed I was being used as a channel for entities on the other side. Many of the messages seemed to come from persons who have walked this earth and experienced the same things we experience in our everyday lives. They come through with a newfound wisdom from the other side, a whole new perspective for us to view and advice on how to pursue our souls' purpose. Most importantly, we must view others as souls on a similar journey as our own, seeking awareness and the realization that this life is not the true life.

Have I accomplished something great? I hesitate to take credit for any of what is found in this book. I merely wrote what popped into my head at particular times and started to pay attention to the thoughts and words we all have floating around in our heads. I believe we are all capable of receiving such inspiring messages if we remain open to all this life contains beyond the material.

Each and every one of us has had an event or events occur that can only be explained as a miracle of sorts. The accident you avoided, the recovery of a loved one, the job you never thought you would get, the children you never thought you would have, or even the life-changing tragedies that somehow revealed to us the better side of people who came to our aid when we were suffering. Almost all of these have occurred in my life, and I failed to see the blessings of these miracles until I started writing this book—a book that has been Divinely influenced.

It is possible that this book is merely an exercise for my benefit only, but I think not. In no way am I insinuating that I have just given you all the answers to life and what life is all about. Instead, I'm sharing with you the, shall I say, cheat sheet that I have been given. My beliefs have turned to a knowing—a knowing that, yes, God will assess how far we have come from our experiences here on earth, and none of us will be condemned provided that we make a conscious effort to include God in our lives.

There was one more message that had to be included in this book, and it arrived on October 5, 2012. When I started writing this book, I wondered how I would know when to end it. I was, and am still, pretty sure the messages will continue, and I left it in God's hands to give me the guidance I needed. Actually, this whole book was guided by His hand, and little of it came from my own effort. The experiences I have spoken of I now see were all orchestrated by God, and the only credit I should receive is that I eventually choose to follow the path being opened up to me. The message on October 5th speaks to all of us about awareness, choice, and even God's thanks to those of us who have chosen to walk in His light. Best of all, this will not be the last message I receive, but it is a great way to end this book and a perfect spot to step onto our walk to eternity.

October 5, 2012

The cloak of darkness that envelops your world must be lifted. For you and those of you who have openly accepted these messages, the blanket of despair, disillusionment, confusion, and questions that wrapped themselves around your existence are being pulled away. Better yet, they are being thrown off by those who have made a choice—the choice to follow the path illuminated by Me. Would it not be easier for Me to appear to the masses and speak the truth? I hear your thoughts.

By now, you and those of you who have received these messages must realize this would not and could not be the way. Have I not shown you My works and explained My ways, and have you not even witnessed events from the Divine only to still question what you have seen or experienced? You specifically, the one assigned the task of writing the messages, still harbor doubt of the validity of what has been written.

It is happening exactly the way it is supposed to. Your world is changing slowly. Is it happening too slow or too fast? This does not matter. Does everyone who reads what has been written believe or not believe? This also does not matter. What matters most is for the ones who choose to believe; they must live their lives in a way that their actions speak louder than their words. Through the actions of a few, many can be saved, and through the actions of many, the masses can be saved.

The saving I speak of is not on the human level; it is on the spiritual level. The saving I speak of is the saving of one from his or her own spiritual blackness in which many in your world reside. Through your actions and the actions of many like you, the darkness can be lifted, and choices can be made clearer for those who cannot see.

As a field of corn is planted one seed at a time, life is lived one step at a time. The awakening your planet needs will occur one soul at a time. Drop a seed of kindness wherever you go, and soon a forest of peace will cover your world. Through this peace will come awareness, acknowledgment, and an awakening to what true and everlasting life is.

My only direction to those who have read these messages is to read them again and place yourself as the one who has received them. Yes, though originally received to personally address a specific event in a specific person's life, the messages are universal to all. Each and every person can see him- or herself in what has been written. This is how the Divine works. What has seemed to be a singular event for a single person speaks volumes to the masses.

I feel joy and happiness for the choice made through the gift of free will when the choice leads you closer to Me. This shows Me what you have become. All will make the choice in this lifetime or other lifetimes, and eventually all will walk in My light—the light that is the true and unconditional love that I have for each and every one of you. This is the same love you too must have for each and every person for your world to survive.

Thankful am I to you; yes, thankful am I to you for the choice you have made to walk in My light and hear My words and the words of others from the Divine.

Joyous has been this reunion and will be the reunion you and I will have in heaven. My hands are upon your shoulders as the tears of joy, love, and peace flow from your eyes. The windows of your soul have been opened, and I have entered. Now go about your day fearless of what tomorrow brings and reflect My light to others.

You must now accept that you are a beacon of My light for others to see. From this point on never doubt, question, or try to validate what you see and believe in regards to the Divine. Without fear, speak of what you have come to know. Without fear, put your words in print.

This is not an ending or a parting of ways. This is a welcome and a joining of souls. You have made a choice to listen, to write, and to believe, and I have made a choice also. I have chosen you to complete this task now and to relax in your newfound awareness.

The messages will not stop and must continue to be received, for the channel has been opened, and nothing in the universe can block a channel opened to My light.

Breathe easy. Relax. I and those of the Divine will return.

Index

A
Ambition, 70
Awakenings, 59–67
Awareness, 35–36, 44–45, 70, 86–87, 90–93, 100–103, 120

C
Catholicism, 3–4
Christmas, 46–47
Comtois, Roland, 15–16

D
Death, xvi, 40, 47, 72, 108
Disappointments, 115–17
Discernment, 2–3
Dreams, 1–5

E
Easter, 72–74
Education, 7–8
Ego, 64, 70
Energy, 10–11, 108–9
Evolvement, 7–11, 53–55, 82–83

F
Faith, renewal of, 39
Fear, 69–87, 106–7

Forgiveness, 1–5, 37–47, 50–53, 75–78, 110–12
Free will, 27–29, 38–47, 65, 97
    choices and, 40–41

G
God
    belief in, 61
    control to, 102–3
    existence of, 95
    faith in, xv
    guidance from, ix, 17, 85–86
    judgment and, 107
    love and, 96–97
    messages from, 14–17, 19–21, 23–25, 37–47, 49–58, 59–67, 69–87, 89–97, 105–17, 119–24
    in our lives, 119–24
    path to heaven and, 11
    patience of, 107
    separation from, 35–36
    vision and wisdom of, 65
Guilt, 4–5

H
Happiness, 101, 123–24
Healing, xiv
Health, xiii–xiv
Heaven, 7–11, 44, 105–6

light of, 13–17
Holidays, 32–35, 44
   Christmas, 46–47
   Easter, 72–74
   Thanksgiving, 32–35

I
Ideals, 80–82
Inspiration, 10–11

J
Jesus, 46–47, 72–74
Judgment, 2–3, 107

K
Knowledge, 114

L
Life
   alternative existence and, 59–67
   as an illusion, 14–15
   awakenings and, 59–67
   awareness of, 35–36, 61–63, 70, 86–87, 90–93, 100–103, 120
   being human and, 23–25
   challenges of, 93
   choices and, 28, 80–82
   chosen path of, 74–75
   clarity of, 49–58
   control to God and, 102–3
   evolution of, 7–11, 53–55, 82–83
   experiences, 55–56
   journey of, 35
   joys of, 111, 123–24
   lessons, 39, 41–42
   obstacles to, 16–17
   perception of, 65–66, 90
   physical world and, 78–79
   purpose of, 20, 71, 90
   quality of, 59–60
   questions about, 56–57
   responsibility and, 55–56
   secret to, 37–39
   simplicity of, 93–94
   trials, tribulations, and problems, 19–21
Love, 4–5, 96–97

M
Marriage, 76–77
Materialism, 9–10, 29, 100–101, 109
Meditation, 7–11, 25, 43–44
Messages, from God, 14–17, 19–21, 23–25, 37–47, 49–58, 59–67, 69–87, 89–97, 105–17, 119–24
Miracles, 122

P
Prayer, 31–36, 67
Pride, 20–21

Q
Qigong, 3

R
Reality, 32, 94–96
Recognition, 45–46
Reincarnation, 3
Religion
   acceptance of, 80–82
   faith in, xi–xii
Responsibility, 55–56

S

Second Coming, 73–74
Self, 23–25, 38–39
    connectedness to other humans, 60
    disappointments and, 115–17
    ego and, 64, 70
    inadequacy of, 101–3
    me first attitude, 97
    purpose of, 94–96
    worth, 100
Shiatsu, 3
Soul, 38–39, 116
Soul mates, 45–46
Spirituality, 7–11, 27–29, 43–47, 73–74, 80–82, 105–17
    mile markers of, 44–47

T

Thanksgiving, 32–35

V

Visions, xvi–xvii, 13–17